THE CRAFT AND THE CROSS

The Craft
and the
Cross

IAN GORDON

KINGSWAY PUBLICATIONS
EASTBOURNE

Biblical quotations are from the
Good News Bible © American Bible Society 1976 and the
New International Version © International Bible Society
1973, 1978, 1984

Cover design by W James Hammond

British Library Cataloguing in Publication Data

Gordon, Ian
    The craft and the cross.
    1. Christianity. Conversion of non-Christians
    I. Title
    248.2'46

ISBN 0-86065-694-2

The accounts in this book are factual, but
in the interests of personal privacy, certain
names and details have been altered.

Printed in Great Britain for
KINGSWAY PUBLICATIONS LTD
1 St Anne's Road, Eastbourne, E Sussex BN21 3UN by
Courier International Ltd, Tiptree, Essex
Typeset by Nuprint Ltd,
30b Station Road, Harpenden, Herts AL5 4SE.

Contents

Acknowledgements 7
1 The Secret and Mysterious Rite 9
2 Gurkhas and Gurus 19
3 Change of Direction 33
4 Climbing the Ladder 43
5 A Realisation of Ambitions 55
6 The Shadow of a Doubt 66
7 A Degree of Christianity? 74
8 Reflections 87
9 The Crashing Blow 91
10 Unexpected Meeting 99
11 Aftermath 106
12 No Danger—God at Work! 121
13 As we forgive those... 133
14 Death of a Passion 145
15 A Search for the Roots 154
16 The Kabbala 167
17 Darkness into Light 180
Bibliography 185

Acknowledgements

In *Truth to Tell* David Pawson wrote 'no book is the work of one person. Even the Author of the Bible was helped by over forty men who turned his words into speech and print.' So also this book is the result of suggestions and prodding by others prompted by God in his unmistakeable way.

In the summer of 1986 at a Full Gospel Businessmen's Fellowship International Convention in Bury St Edmunds, the International Director for UK, John Wright, who had so generously enabled Sally and me to be there in the first place, urged me to write this book.

Within a few weeks Clive Calver, General Secretary of the Evangelical Alliance, completely unsolicited, voiced the same sentiments 120 miles away in Mayfield and a little later I was contacted by Kingsway Publications in East-bourne.

The task of setting down coherently on paper the mass of knowledge of all sorts that I had acquired through months of reading and listening to tapes proved so daunting that for a long time I shrank from it. Finally, in the early Summer of 1988, assistance was provided in truly remarkable circumstances and it was so apparent that God wanted this book written that, amid much prayer and encouragement from my beloved brothers and sisters in

Christ at Colkins Mill Church, Mayfield, in June 1988 events eventually got under way.

It is no exaggeration to say that without Polly Bradford my garrulous and rambling array of verbal and written jottings would never have appeared in relevant, coherent and readable prose. My heartfelt thanks go to her for her patience with my constant stream of suggestions and counter-suggestions, her tact, discernment and dogged obedience to God to ensure only what is relevant has ultimately been written, and her skill not only with words but also with the word processor, thus saving me the drudgery of hours of single finger tapping at a typewriter.

Especially my gratitude, thanks and admiration go to my wife, Sally, who patiently over many years put up with a man doggedly set on a road of personal ambition driven by pride, conceit, arrogance and self-centredness. She had found Jesus earlier in her life and for sixteen years her constant devoted intercession on my behalf finally bore fruit in circumstances described within these pages. In that time she bore me four super children who in spite of great efforts on their part could never get near to the man who is supposed to be their father. He was too busy, often away from home, worshipping Mammon and Molech.

We now have a marriage and a family as a result of Sally's love, loyalty, devotion and obedience to our heavenly Father and the children have a father with time and desire to share a life that now is focused and centred on Jesus, the Lord of our lives.

Finally and most importantly, my thanks go to Jesus himself who, in answer to Sally's constant beseeching, finally decided that drastic measures were needed to get my attention. His constant love and protection throughout my life, bringing me safely through a multitude of hairraising escapades, had failed to evoke any response from me. What he did is described in the story that follows.

IAN GORDON

I

The Secret and Mysterious Rite

I was in total darkness, the soft cloth of the blindfold successfully obscuring everything from my view. As I felt the noose being placed around my neck, a sense of acute apprehension came over me and in the split second before common sense gained the upper hand, images of scaffolds and executioners flashed across my mind. The sensation, though brief, was utterly horrible and I began to wonder what on earth I had let myself in for. I recalled the words I had heard earlier, spoken by one man after another.

'Don't worry,' each had said, 'We've all been through it.'

Standing there now, my clothing in disarray, completely sightless, those encouraging expressions took on a new and altogether more sinister significance. What exactly was it, this ordeal I had to go through? Before my imagination really got into gear I took a deep breath and immediately felt calmer.

'After all,' I reasoned with myself, 'if all these people, men you work with, whose judgment you trust, decent men, family men, have all undergone this before you, it can't be so very terrible...can it?'

I wasn't left too long to wonder. I heard three knocks, followed by three more, this time much nearer. I've heard it said that if you are deprived of one of your senses, another will become highly developed by way of compensation, and certainly in the time of my artificial blindness I was acutely aware of the sounds around me, so that when a voice suddenly spoke fairly close to me I gave a nervous start. I heard the words 'How does he hope to obtain those privileges?' and another voice, this time familiar to me, answered 'By the help of God, being free and of good report.'

'Halt,' came the reply, 'while I report to the Worshipful Master.'

The sound of a door closing. A minute of silence while I strained to catch any sound that would give me a clue as to what was happening. The door opening. I didn't move. I felt a sharp prick on my left, bared breast and my hand was taken in a firm grip. The familiar voice spoke into my ear: 'When I say, step off with the left foot. Don't say anything unless I prompt you. Now, step!'

I took a pace forward. This was it. My initiation was about to begin.

A short time earlier, my friend and colleague, Hamish Morrison, had met me, as arranged, at the Rostrum in Lloyd's, where we both worked at the time, and together we made our way across Lime Street and into what was then known as the Old Lloyd's Building. I was looking forward to the evening ahead with a pleasurable anticipation heightened by a sense of the unknown. Some weeks earlier I had received my 'summons' to this May meeting of Lutine Lodge when I would be initiated into Freemasonry as an Entered Apprentice. Hamish had proposed me, another colleague seconded the proposal and now the moment had arrived.

I had meticulously followed my instructions regarding dress, and as we entered the Old Building I noticed several others attired in similar fashion to Hamish and myself, in dark suits, white shirts, black ties and black shoes and socks. We all made our way to the Old Committee Room which was situated on one of the upper floors. It was my first entry into the Old Building and I glanced about me curiously as I followed Hamish from the rickety lift, along the corridor towards the Committee Room. He ushered me into what appeared to be a sort of ante-room and handed me over into the care of someone whom he introduced as 'The Tyler'. The room began to fill with men, some of whom I knew either by name or sight, and all acknowledged my presence in a friendly way. Several greeted me warmly, using various terms of encouragement, including the phrase I was soon to recollect—'Don't worry, now. We've all been through it, you know.' The Tyler approached, smiling.

'Now this is where you have to leave us for a moment or two. You mustn't see anything that would spoil things for you.'

Intrigued, I allowed myself to be confined to a small storeroom from where I could hear the others talking quietly and laughing with each other. Soon all was quiet and the Tyler appeared to release me from my cupboard. Back in the lobby, I noticed various coats, briefcases and so forth which had been left about, then from somewhere close at hand an organ began to play and voices were raised in a hymn. For all the world I might have been in the vestry of a church. I looked inquiringly at my companion. He smiled but said nothing. The singing ceased and I heard banging, like the sound of an auctioneer's hammer being brought down fairly forcefully. Again I glanced at the Tyler. His smile broadened.

'You'll soon find out what everything is,' he assured me.

There were two doors in the room, one from the corridor, and another which I assumed led into the Committee Room itself. This door now opened and a head popped round and addressed the Tyler with the words 'Ballot OK'. With the by now familiar smile of reassurance at me, it withdrew.

'Good,' said the Tyler. 'Now we can get ready.'

Today there are few, if any, undisclosed secrets regarding masonic ritual, but in 1974, at the time of my initiation into the organisation which members call The Craft, I knew virtually nothing, so I was somewhat taken aback by the instructions I now received. However, I entered into the spirit of the evening and, with my curiosity well and truly aroused, obligingly removed jacket and tie and handed over all the metal objects which I had about me, including watch, cuff-links and cash. I unbuttoned my shirt and the Tyler arranged it so as to expose my left breast. I rolled up my right shirt-sleeve to above the elbow, and my left trouser-leg to above the knee.

Now I have to admit that at this point in the proceedings I was beginning to feel just the tiniest bit foolish, and as my right shoe was removed and replaced with a backless slipper, I couldn't help being glad that there was no full-length mirror in the room!

'What on earth is this all about?' I was asking myself as the soft cloth was placed over my eyes and made secure. This was followed by the silken noose, and it was at that moment that my half-amused interest suddenly gave way to a quite unexpected sense of apprehension.

I do not propose to record here every detail of the ensuing ceremony. These masonic rituals are no longer part of the great unknown, and anyone who wishes may learn the precise format very easily from previously published works on the subject. For me the whole procedure which followed from the moment I stepped out blindly on my left foot, my hand gripped firmly by an unseen officer of the Lodge, was a completely strange experience.

Wearing a blindfold for any length of time has a remarkably disorientating effect, as anyone will recall who has played the children's game of Blind Man's Bluff. I knew that we had entered the Committee Room but I had no sense of the room's size or of the number of people in it. A disembodied voice put questions to me and the responses were whispered in my ear for me to repeat aloud. I knelt, I stood, I was led around the room, turning squarely as we changed direction as I was told to do, and eventually was brought back to a stationary position, but by this time had no way of knowing whether it was my original starting point or not! Obeying all the instructions given me, I felt my hand being placed on what was referred to as 'The Volume of the Sacred Law'. Into my left hand was put a cold metallic object which I guessed, correctly as it turned out, was a pair of compasses, and in this position, kneeling, one hand on the book with the point of the compasses pointing towards me, I took my first masonic oath.

The vows or 'obligations' which a candidate has to make as he progresses through the degrees of the Craft, increase in bloodthirstiness and melodrama at each stage. By comparison with later ones the penal clause repeated by the Entered Apprentice seems fairly mild, but at the time the idea of having my 'throat cut across, my tongue torn out by the root and buried in the sand at low water mark' if I ever betrayed any secrets, caused a very real chill to pass through me. It was, of course, no worse than the type of schoolboy threats and promises which many of us experienced in 'secret society' games as children, but in that unseen room, with a noose around my neck and my hand on what I assumed to be the Bible, as in a Court of Law, there was an air of gravity and a suggestion of seriousness which seemed a world away from childhood games.

Eventually I heard these words:

'Having been kept for a considerable time in a state of darkness, what in your present situation is the predominant wish of your heart?'

'Light,' I replied, as firmly as I could. The voice spoke again, quite near me. There was a bang such as I had heard earlier, a clapping of many hands and my blindfold was smoothly removed. I blinked. Something was shielding my eyes so that they focused immediately on a Bible which lay open in front of me. I blinked again, trying hard to adjust to what seemed a brilliant light, and as the noose was removed from around my neck I found myself looking into the smiling face of the Worshipful Master of Lutine Lodge, whom I recognised as a colleague and friend of Hamish Morrison, with whom I had frequently enjoyed a chat over coffee after lunch in Lloyd's.

This was my first sight of masonic regalia, and very attractive it was I thought, as I took in the wide shawl collar of pale blue watered silk and the white apron trimmed with the same blue. From the collar hung some sort of angular pendant and on his left lapel he wore an impressive blue and gold medal. I was later able to study the Worshipful Master's dress in more detail, and still later of course, the significance of each piece became clear, but in those moments after my vision was restored I was really mainly aware of the considerable effort my colleague was putting into remembering the correct words while at the same time trying to put the new and rather nervous candidate before him at his ease. The Master has a very large 'part' to learn in the drama of such ceremonies, and although he may have a prompt, his role can make or mar the proceedings for the initiate. The seriousness with which my colleague took his role was obvious from the fact that the poor man was perspiring freely!

I tried to follow the words he was now addressing to me. He helped me to rise from my kneeling position and explained to me the significance of the noose, which he called a cable-tow, and of the dagger which I now realised had caused the sharp prick on my chest which I had felt at the outset. In theory at least, the noose, had I decided to run away there and then, would have strangled me, and the dagger, had I moved forward too quickly, could have pierced my chest. Theory only of course, but with the memory of the noose and the oath still fresh in my mind, I was thankful that I had taken the Tyler's instructions seriously and obeyed them to the letter.

As my initiation ceremony continued I was able to take in something of my surroundings. The Committee Room was large and well-proportioned with the dark oak panelling of the Jacobean period. On the polished floor was a black and white carpet, chequered like a chessboard, and it was around this carpet that I had been led, being displayed, as it were, to the members of the Lodge who were seated around it. I was conducted around it again as the proceedings continued, answering with prompting all the questions put to me.

At last I returned to the Worshipful Master, having been presented with my first masonic apron, a plain white garment made from lambskin and without any form of decoration. I was then given a Book of Constitutions and a Volume of By-Laws which I was told to peruse. I was shown a Charter and also a set of working tools, comprising gauge, gavel and chisel, and their masonic significance was explained. (I will discuss this in detail in a later chapter.) Eventually I received the instruction to 'retire and restore yourself to your personal comforts', after which I saluted the Master with the newly-learned sign, and then was escorted back to the lobby where the Tyler had prepared me earlier—centuries earlier it seemed! He was still smiling and congratulated me on my entry into the Craft.

As I fastened my shirt and resumed my normal appearance, I couldn't escape a sensation of relief that it was all over. Part of me was slightly ashamed of my earlier nervousness, but the memory of the noose and the dagger, and the macabre terms of the oath were still in my mind. It is easy to be confident and self-assured in the bright light of day, but in the dark, dealing with the unknown, all the nameless fears of childhood can steal in and take over the mind of the sanest and most balanced adult.

The Tyler helped me secure my apron, then after another series of knocks and responses, I was conducted back into the Committee Room and given my position in the Lodge at the end of the chequered carpet opposite the Master. Listening to the address which followed, which was in essence a charge on me to live to a high moral standard based on the Volume of the Sacred Law, I felt a sense of accomplishment, of satisfaction. Whatever this organisation might be, and I was just starting to discover something of it, I was glad to be a part of it. I looked around at my fellow-masons, and a sense of belonging came over me, of belonging to a good society which was peopled with good men who did good things. I did not trouble to define to myself precisely what I meant by the term 'good' at that time in my life.

I have said that my knowledge of the Craft was at this time very scanty, but as the Master went on to deliver an address of explanation, I began to get some sense of what I can only call the solidity of the movement. Freemasonry purports to originate in the building of King Solomon's temple, which is related in the Bible, in the First Book of Kings and the Second Book of Chronicles. Thus all ritual and regalia are based on the concept of design and construction, with God being referred to as the Great Architect of the Universe. These two notions, that is, basic Old Testament scripture and the construction of something as vast and enduring as a temple, seemed together to induce in me an aggreeable sense of correctness, of secure foundations and great strength. These were the impressions which formed in my mind on that first evening, and when we rose at the end of the ceremonies, I joined in the closing hymn with unalloyed enthusiasm.

As we followed the Worshipful Master and the other officers from the room, the atmosphere became more relaxed. In the lobby, where we changed out of our masonic dress, my hand was shaken innumerable times and words of congratulation and welcome filled my ears. There was a tremendous feeling of warmth and camaraderie and for the first time I really began to relax and enjoy myself. Several times I was told that this was my evening and I must be sure to enjoy it, one instruction which I fully intended to follow!

Anyone who remembers the old Lloyd's will recall the Coffee Room which was in effect the social hub of the building. It was there that I had often sat and chatted with Hamish and other colleagues over a drink, and it was to that room that we were now heading. As I entered, Hamish met me with congratulations and a large gin and tonic. I took a sizeable swallow.

'I needed that!' I said, only half in jest, and Hamish laughed.

'We've all been through it,' he said.

'So I've been told,' I replied with feeling, 'and now I know exactly what "it" is!'

I was introduced to many new 'brothers'. Some I had come across frequently in Lloyd's, others I knew scarcely at all, but now I felt a new sense of comradeship and goodwill. We passed through the swing doors into the Captain's Room and took our places at the long table where we were served a splendid dinner. In the words of the song, the wine was good, the food was good, the company was great. As I leaned back in my chair, a glass of excellent brandy in my hand, I felt that life was rather good for Ian Gordon. Had anyone told me then that in a few short years my business career would be in ruins and I would be in a frame of mind to commit murder, I would have labelled him drunk or lunatic, or both.

2

Gurkhas and Gurus

I have often been asked why I became a Freemason in the first place and what I think is the attraction of the Craft. The first part of the question is easily, if tritely, answered by saying that, like most things we choose to do in life, it seemed like a good idea at the time. The second part is infinitely more complex. Freemasonry seems to represent different things to different people; in my case it combined the all-male camaraderie which I had enjoyed at public school and later in the regimental mess, with the esoteric enjoyment of an exclusive club, all tempered by a good helping of firmly-based, old-fashioned religion.

There has been much discussion during the past few years on the question of whether or not Freemasonry sets itself up as a religion, and this is something which I shall deal with in a later chapter. Some would claim that it makes no attempt at all to offer an alternative to orthodoxy, but I know that for me, at the time, it met a need in my spiritual life, as well as forming a logical extension to my business and social life.

Prior to entering the Craft, my knowledge of it was scanty. My mother had given me the idea that masons were 'good' men, people to be admired and emulated; her father was a lifelong Freemason and also a devout Anglican, and she herself had been taught conventional values, though with debatable success, as all her life was spent rebelling against most of them. She rejected the doctrines of the Anglican church and embarked on her own search for truth, and my father, though a chorister in his youth, had by the time of my birth, abandoned church-going entirely.

I was born in Penang, Malaya, as World War Two entered its second year, and when Singapore eventually fell, my father, who by then had been drafted into the Singapore Volunteers, was captured by the Japanese and interned in the infamous Changi gaol, before being transported north to work on the even more notorious Burma Railway. My mother and I were evacuated to India, getting out on the last ship to leave Singapore before the island surrendered. We were to spend three-and-a-half years in India before returning to England some time between VE and VJ Day, and my earliest memories are of heat and brilliant colour, noise, and strange, pungent smells. I was too young to realise what a difficult time this was for my mother and the other women evacuees. Although they were very much the lucky ones in that they had escaped from the Japanese, they had, almost without exception, had to leave all their possessions behind and consequently arrived in India as penniless refugees. However, all this meant nothing to me, and until I was nearly five years old, India was the only home I knew.

Happily, my father survived the war and eventually returned to his former occupation in Singapore. I was sent off to prep school near Perth, Western Australia, and it was there that I first made the acquaintance of formal religion. Each Sunday we made the pilgrimage from the Junior School to the Senior School Chapel to take part in the service led by Canon Freith, a gentle if rather august man, who was Headmaster of the school. That walk across the school grounds seemed very long, the chapel vast, high and austere, and as for God himself, to a seven-year-old who was missing the mother he had had to leave with a father he scarcely knew, God was every bit as unreachable as the high chapel ceiling. I certainly didn't spend much time thinking about him; the Sunday Service was just another part of the school curriculum; it belonged with maths and geography and the rest. I had to attend it just as I had to attend my other classes; it was all part of school life.

When I was despatched back to England to continue my education at a Surrey prep school, I found little or no difference, except that the chapel was smaller and cosier (or had I merely grown so much in two years?) and I had begun to enjoy the musical content of the services to the extent that I became a willing member of the choir. We continued to study 'Scripture' but it was still just another subject on a crowded curriculum. Certainly nobody ever tried talking to me or, as far as I know, to any of us on a more intimate or pastoral level. Not that I particularly wanted that; God was still just God, up there somewhere, very remote, to be addressed with due reverence at morning assemblies and chapel services.

He was not brought any nearer by my experiences at home during the holidays. My mother, who had been strongly influenced by the Eastern religions which she had encountered during our stay in India, was well into her quest for the Universal Truth, and was at this time totally enraptured by a book called 'Van Loon's Lives'. This contained the numerous and highly complex opinions of one Henrik William Van Loon as to the origins and meaning of life. Everything Christian was an anathema to her, and she would expound at great length to me, a captive audience, on the theories of this Van Loon and others. By the time I entered Charterhouse School at the age of thirteen, and then throughout my teens, I was absorbing, albeit unconsciously, a wide variety of philosophical ideas as well as traditional Anglican doctrine.

The prospect of Confirmation began to loom, and I rebelled. The whole thing seemed devoid of meaning to me. I knew that many of my contemporaries would be submitting to the ritual only because of the insistence of parents or godparents, without any real understanding or commitment on their own part, and I was not prepared to go along with a hollow ceremony just for the sake of appearances. I was certainly under no family pressure myself, for although my parents had observed the conventions by having me baptised in Saint Andrew's Cathedral, Singapore, I never knew any godparents, and by the time of my Confirmation, my parents' relationship had deteriorated to a point where they barely communicated with each other.

This was a period of great personal unhappiness for me, but I did not consider God to be someone I could look to for comfort and strength. I did believe that there was some kind of deity, but that it was a vague, universal being whom all religions of the world worshipped under different names. The idea of a personal God living within me was something which never entered my head and I would have found the notion incomprehensible.

It was through the influence of my house-master that I finally came round to accepting the idea of Confirmation. A very gentle and loving man, Richard Fletcher, or Dickie F as he was known by his disrespectful charges, spent a lot of time talking to me and discussing my misgivings. He was a man for whom I felt a good deal of affection and respect. He understood the trying time I was going through during the disintegration of my parents' marriage, and while I can't say that I regarded him as a substitute for my father, I certainly saw him as an intermediary, even a barrier, between the two of us.

My father had physically survived his internment under

the Japanese, but like many others who had endured the ordeal, he had been irreparably damaged emotionally and mentally by his treatment. This manifested itself in violent changes of mood and he would be transformed, almost in a moment, from an apparently normal, loving father into a terrifyingly unrecognisable monster of violence. I was more fortunate than my younger brothers and sister in that I was away at boarding school for most of the year, while they, living at home, had to bear the brunt of my father's conduct. Nevertheless, the effect on me during those years was profound, and Richard Fletcher did his best to provide a steadying influence in my life and to act as a caring confidant when needed. It was mostly out of respect for him that I eventually agreed to be confirmed. I believed that he knew what was best for me and although he was invariably gentle in his approach I, being a normally obnoxious teenager, couldn't help also being swayed by the prospect of getting him off my back!

So I was duly confirmed by the Bishop of Portsmouth, my only gesture of defiance against the system being to ignore the 'No Hair-oil to be worn' rule. Like many of my fellow candidates, transgressors all, I was liberal with the Brylcreem, and had the satisfaction of seeing His Grace's hand grow greasier and greasier as the ceremony progressed. Poor man; but he may have come to expect it as one of the hazards of his calling!

As far as I was concerned I was now a bona-fide Christian, in name at least, baptised and confirmed into the Anglican Communion, and I continued to take part in the school services with increasing enjoyment though it was not enjoyment of a spiritual kind. Charterhouse School Chapel is a vast place, but was aesthetically very pleasing to me in its unadorned simplicity, and I found a good deal of satisfaction in giving full voice, along with eight hundred others, in great ecclesiastical singalongs. Summer

Evensong was the service which I enjoyed most, and as well as my liking for church music, I had begun to develop a taste for ritual which was to remain with me in later life.

I had heard and read enough of the New Testament to form certain expectations of what Christian living ought to be, and I began at this time to experience feelings of distaste for what I saw as hypocrisy in certain quarters. I had before me in Richard Fletcher, and in his successor George Ullyott, examples of what I considered real Christian lifestyle. I was fortunate in both my house-masters; these men daily put their beliefs into practice in their attitude to pupils and colleagues. I was not surprised when 'Dickie F' left Charterhouse to become headmaster, not of a smart prep or public school, but of a school for deaf and dumb children. Even as an averagely insensitive youth I could appreciate how that role would allow him more scope to serve his fellow man.

His successor, George Ullyott, took up his mantle in every way and when I contrasted the conduct of these two men with what I saw around me, that contrast was marked indeed. There is some excuse for immature young men having double standards with one norm for church behaviour and another for the rest of the week, but I found it difficult to admire much in the habits of the school's 'official Christians', that is the chaplains who led our worship each Sunday. One of these men was very fond of hurling chalk and board-rubbers (the wooden-backed variety) from one end of the formroom to the other if he considered someone was paying insufficient attention to his lesson, and in chapel his performance was, shall we say, interesting. He would stand in the pulpit, hands clasped to his chest, eyes closed, raising his face heavenwards one minute and feetwards the next and deliver a sermon which comprised of inaudible mutterings interspersed with explosive but incomprehensible exhortations. We found the whole thing somewhat hypnotic in its

dreadfulness and it did very little to bring anyone nearer
to the reality of God.

Thus I found myself very much in the position of
onlooker, forming conclusions, pronouncing judgements
and on the whole dismissing religion as I had so far experienced it, as empty and dead, devoid of sincerity but not
bad fun as regards the music and the spectacle.

This attitude was reinforced during my time at the
Royal Military Academy, Sandhurst. I left Charterhouse
without a clue as to what I was going to do with my life.
My parents were by then separated, and various members
of the family thought it would be a good idea for me to
join the Army. I had no strong feelings on the subject, so I
enlisted as a private soldier in the Queen's Own Royal
West Kent Regiment and after six months, having decided
that the life would suit me, I duly entered Sandhurst as an
officer-cadet.

Where Sundays at school had been dominated by attendance at Chapel, they were now centred around Church
Parade, and this made very much the same impression on
me, that is, hardly any. I enjoyed, as always, the spectacle
of it; the highest standards of dress and presentation were
demanded, not so much because of going into the presence of God, but more because exemplary appearance
was expected of us at all times as future officers in the
British Army. I had no qualms about the ethics of taking
up arms. Having been fairly lukewarm about a service
career, I found, once an officer-cadet, that I was caught up
in the whole charisma of military life. I considered it a
noble thing to fight and if necessary to die for one's
country, and I would sit in the chapel reading on the
marble columns the lists of names of those who had died
in action and admiring the courage of these men.

God, of course, would always be on the side of the just,
that is the British, and I identified strongly with Shake-
speare's Henry the Fifth, with his 'God for England,

Harry and Saint George': I emerged from my training believing firmly in the superiority of the British Officer Class and in the existence of a Deity who was primarily concerned with, and approachable via, the Church of England, but who was at least accessible to other races throughout the world who worshipped him in different ways and under different names.

In December 1960, eight days before my twentieth birthday, I was commissioned into the First Battalion 6th Queen Elizabeth's Own Gurkha Rifles, and after six months training in England, embarked with four brother-officers, all newly-commissioned, on board the SS Nevasa on our way to join our regiments in the Far East, in my case in Kluang, Malaya.

I enjoyed my years of service in the Brigade of Gurkhas. They truly are a remarkable breed of men, mostly Hindu, and partly because I respected them a great deal, and partly out of interest, I took the opportunity of learning what I could about their religion. We had a regimental priest, a Brahmin, and the British officers were expected to participate in the religious festivals which occurred at frequent intervals. This certainly involved no hardship for me; with my liberal Anglican attitude I found no conflict of conscience. To me these people were merely worshipping God in their own way, and if that incorporated some rather quaint customs such as animal sacrifice, well, the Old Testament was full of similar stuff, wasn't it?

The Gurkhas really knew how to celebrate a religious festival to the full and I shared their pleasure. I loved the spectacle and the ritual, not to mention the excessive eating and drinking which seemed to form an intrinsic part of each one. The contrast between the vibrant worship of the Hindus, or the Muslims of Malaya's indigenous population, and the restrained formality of Christianity struck me forcibly. During my time in the Far East I scarcely entered a Christian gathering; occasionally a priest would visit to celebrate Communion, and there was sometimes the wedding of a brother-officer to attend, but my years with the Gurkhas, instead of being punctuated by Christmas, Easter, Whitsuntide and so forth, ran comfortably along from one Hindu festival to the next and I looked forward to them all. The only one which took a little will-power and a lot of alcohol to survive was the longest one of these. In late summer or early autumn, depending upon the position of the stars, the great Dashera festival took place, which included the renowned head-chopping session. At some point during the nine or ten days of celebration, when the priests agreed it was auspicious, this sacrificial slaughter began. Live chickens and goats were decapitated and the whole gory procedure culminated in the beheading of a buffalo by means of a single blow from the great double-handed Kukhri, the ceremonial knife.

It was a great honour for the Gurkha soldier who was chosen to carry out this task, and the responsibility was equally great; tradition held that failure to sever the head at one stroke would mean bad luck for the regiment for the coming year. The first time I saw this I watched with mingled horror and fascination as the poor beast was tethered by the head to the ceremonial chopping-post, and its neck stretched out ready for the blow. In my years there I saw only one failure. When my battalion was posted to Britain such customs were regarded as barbaric, and were forbidden at the instigation of the RSPCA and the animal-loving British public, so our second battalion left in the Far East would carry out the ritual on behalf of their brothers in the United Kingdom, thus ensuring the continuing prosperity of the regiment.

The obvious enthusiasm for fervent worship which the Gurkhas displayed during their festivals impressed me, but when I stopped, as I occasionally did, to consider the implications of their faith, I found no more to satisfy me than I had in my days at school. Hindus, I had found, were as capable as Christians of on the one hand exemplary conduct in the presence of their priest, of lusty participation in a festival or service, and on the other hand, of returning without a thought to an uncaring or worse lifestyle at other times. Nothing I had seen of Islam, either, had induced me to believe that Muslims were any different. It was only when I was posted to Nepal in the spring of 1966 that I discovered a people who came anywhere near meeting my expectations that life should reflect the religious belief that we profess.

Tibet at that time had been overrun by the Chinese, and Nepal, with India, had extended hospitality to thousands of Buddhist refugees. In the main they were despised by the local populace. Nepal, like India, has a strong, multi-tiered caste system; we recruited our troops from the middle tiers, the warrior castes, and the poor Tibetans were regarded as many times lower than the lowest caste Nepalese. I found this a great source of irritation as I, like many others before and since, became immediately enchanted with these gentle people. In contrast with the excitable and sometimes rather bloodthirsty Hindus, they seemed to exude an aura of tranquillity and love, refusing to kill any living thing, and spreading their joy and peace to all around them.

During my two years in Nepal I spent more time than ever before in thinking about God and his identity. I would have claimed to be a Christian; after all, wasn't I confirmed in the Anglican faith? But for that matter, so were millions of others and it did not seem to make any more difference in their lives than it had in mine. My attitude to life and to my fellow creatures was conditioned more by my upbringing than by any religious convictions. My mother had done her best to pass on to me the Victorian standards which her parents had tried to impress on her, exhorting me to tell the truth always, to show good manners to everyone and to be especially considerate to women. I can't say that either of us would have satisfied my grandparents' expectations; as an adult I had come to realise that truth as my mother saw it had a very elastic quality, and as for my behaviour towards women, I had been so affected by what I had seen of my parents' conduct towards each other that I found it very difficult to relate to most women on anything but the most superficial level. To put it bluntly, I was an emotional mess and this frequently resulted in gauche or unfeeling treatment of girlfriends. Whether I measured up to these standards or not, I considered them such that even the most profane aetheist might live decently by. Hindus, Muslims and Chinese Taoists seemed no better and no worse than Christians, but the Buddhist Tibetans were a race apart and I was drawn to them as to a breath of air on an oppressive day.

This was the time, in the late 1960s, of the hippy movement amongst the youth of the Western world, and many young people, mainly Americans, were living in Nepal. They mostly worked with the few missionaries who were there, or with the Peace Corps and United Nations Missions in caring for the refugees and helping agricultural development. So-called civilisation had scarcely penetrated this beautiful country, and for entertainment we had to rely on good old-fashioned conversation. We spent hour after hour in the evenings exchanging ideas and opinions on every subject under the sun including very frequently the question of religious beliefs. It was a strange and significant period in my life, this twenty-two months spent on the roof of the world amongst an incredibly varied group of people. There were three British Army officers, including myself, the Gurkha troops under our command, who were of the Hindu warrior caste, other Hindus ranging from the high-caste Brahmins to the low-

caste untouchables, the Tibetan Buddhist refugees, penniless and despised by their hosts but remaining at peace
with all, and the foreign helpers, mostly middle-class and
idealistic, who were disillusioned with Western society
and its values and were searching for something more
meaningful.

I myself was not consciously searching at that time, but
the endless discussion and argument had caused me to
take stock of my beliefs and I found that I had become
something of a syncretist, selecting and fusing various
concepts of God from all the religions I had come across
and ending up with something which I found I could
accept. This something was still a kind of Universal Deity
and although I wasn't entirely clear where Jesus fitted into
the scheme of things, he was certainly tied up firmly in my
concepts. I didn't know whether I'd got it right or not, but
I didn't consider it vitally important at that stage. To me
the Buddhists seemed to have the right ideas about life,
and any time that I could spend in talking to them or just
being around them, I valued greatly.

One experience in particular affected me deeply and
remains still clear in my mind. I was spending a few
months at the British Gurkha Pension Paying Post up in
the Himalayan foothills at a place called Pokhara. We
closed the Post at about three o'clock each afternoon and
then I had some free time. One of the things I liked to do
was to walk a mile or so up the valley to where one of the
refugee camps was sited and there I would involve myself
with trying to teach a little English to the Tibetans, or
sometimes just amuse myself by joining some of the young
Peace Corps workers in trying to teach the Tibetan children the basic skills of football, that is European style
soccer. This, I might say, was much more difficult than
language teaching: The children had been brought up in
what was virtually a non-competitive environment, so that
the idea of winning or losing was totally alien to them.

Their pleasure in the game was derived solely from running about after the ball—goals were a complete irrelevance.

On one day like this, I was walking through the camp when one of the young Americans pointed out a particular hut which he said was being used for a time by a visiting Lama, a Buddhist priest. This man was reputed to be an emissary from the Dalai Lama himself who was in exile in Dharamsala, in India, and had been sent with others to the various refugee camps to bring comfort and spiritual counsel to the scattered exiles. His presence there, representing a direct link with their spiritual leader, meant a great deal to the Tibetans and I was filled with a curiosity to meet this priest.

I approached the entrance to the hut and tentatively pulled aside the thin curtain; the interior was illuminated only by a shaft of sunlight from one small window high in the opposite wall, and in the dimness I could just make out a figure at the far end of the small room. I took a step inside and my eyes gradually became accustomed to the gloom. The Lama was sitting in the traditional cross-legged position on a rush mat which covered part of the earth floor. His head was shaven and he was wearing a saffron-coloured robe. He smiled, a gentle, peaceful smile which encouraged me to approach and I sat down opposite him. We studied each other in silence. It was difficult to tell his age but his kind eyes seemed to hold the wisdom of the centuries. I knew only about half a dozen words of Tibetan, and the Lama knew no English or Nepalese, but somehow we seemed to communicate with one another and although I was in the hut for only ten minutes or so, I had the most extraordinary sensation of having held a long conversation with him. I emerged into the brilliant sunshine, feeling that I had been in the presence of a 'man of God', that is, this vague Universal Deity who existed within my frame of reference. I felt that I had vicariously experienced some of the peace which comes from being at peace with oneself and in harmony with all creation. I did not feel any envy for this man, no longing to find a similar peace for myself. I was happy with my life as a soldier and felt no desire to emulate the Lamas of this world. What I did feel, however, was a profound admiration for someone who fulfilled so thoroughly his role in life. To me he seemed exactly what a priest ought to be, and the people he had come to comfort and encourage in their exile also seemed to live their faith in a way that no other religion I had yet encountered came anywhere near doing.

3

Change of Direction

In December 1967 my twenty-two months tour of duty in Nepal came to an end and I returned to the United Kingdom for a long leave. On the long flight home I let my mind dwell luxuriously on the many things I had to look forward to in the coming months. I was longing to see England again after my prolonged absence and I was really hoping for a good summer with all its traditional pleasures, particularly the cricket, a sport which I have always loved. I was anxious to see my mother who had suffered a serious heart attack earlier that year. She had made a good recovery and had begun a new life for herself. My father had died the previous year, having lived apart from my mother for a long time, and she had settled in Henley-on-Thames where she had opened an employment agency. I was hoping that by the time I came back on leave she would have made lots of social contacts, a wish that was not entirely altruistic, because above all I wanted to have some fun during my time at home. I was in the mood to meet lots of pretty girls and generally have a good time.

It was dark when we finally landed at Heathrow and as I was driven from the airport towards Henley, I felt my pleasant sense of anticipation begin to wane a little. Lots of things had changed in my absence, of course, and the greatest surprise was the tremendous increase in traffic. The M4 motorway had been built and I found myself becoming totally unnerved by the continuous flash of headlights as I peered through the driving rain. I felt as though I had been plunged into another world; in Nepal the pace of life had scarcely altered since the 1930s, a very far cry from the England of the late '60s.

My return to England coincided with my youngest brother Graham's Passing Out Parade at Sandhurst. John, the middle brother, had already been commissioned into the 2nd King Edward VII's Own Gurkha Rifles, and Graham was joining the Gurkha Signals.

After Christmas the English winter arrived with a vengeance and I was glad to lie late in bed each morning before facing the rigours of another freezing day. One chilly day towards the end of January I called into my mother's office to find her talking to a pretty dark-haired girl whom she introduced as the daughter of a friend living nearby in Henley. Her name was Sally and she had tired of working in London with the attendant horrors of commuting and had asked my mother to find her something locally. We made pleasant small talk over coffee and later that afternoon I rang my mother on impulse and asked for Sally's telephone number. After all, I'd intended to meet some girls and this seemed a good enough beginning. So I thought!

Sally accepted my somewhat casual invitation to dinner and we drove up to town in my newly-acquired Jaguar, of which I was very proud. I had booked a table at Quaglino's and when I told Sally where we were going she was amused at the coincidence as her grandfather had been a member of 'Quag's' when it was a private club before the war. We had a splendid evening and before it was over I knew beyond any doubt that this was the person with whom I wanted to spend the rest of my life.

So much for my intention to meet as many girls as possible!

Sally too recognised that something very significant had happened, but being much more sensible than I, suggested we take things rather more slowly than I would have wished. She told her mother about my sudden arrival on the scene and introduced us that same week, but her stepfather, who was an officer in the Royal Air Force, had just left England for a tour of duty in the Far East so it was three weeks before he returned to find a strange young man practically resident in his house and obviously totally besotted by his stepdaughter. He took it very well, all things considered, even the fact that I was in the Army, of all unspeakable things, but it was a month or so before Sally and her mother decided it was safe for me to declare my intentions: We became officially engaged and decided on August for our wedding.

From then on Sally and I, not unnaturally, spent all our spare time together. She was working all day but we met for lunch whenever we could, and every evening. Many evenings were spent at my mother's flat. Sally and I were both conscious of the limited time I had to see my mother, who had hardly expected to have to share her eldest son with a fiancée so early in his leave, so the three of us were frequently together. My mother saw no reason to alter her usual topic of conversation, that being her quest for Universal Truth. It seemed to me that she had dabbled in just about every sect and cult in existence and at that point she was deeply into astrology, with all that entailed. She subscribed to a magazine called 'Prediction' and had become very well versed in the whole business of horoscopes and fortune-telling. She had also formed strong connections with practitioners of witchcraft in and around Oxfordshire. Mother, being mother, firmly declared it to be white magic and would extol its virtues at great length, together with much information about spirits and the supernatural.

During our long discussions, it became evident to me that my mother, in her search for truth, had done something very similar to what I myself had done, albeit unconsciously, with my religious belief. She had selected whichever ideas appealed to her from all the varied cults and traditions which she had investigated, most of them Eastern in origin, while I had absorbed a little of each of the Eastern religions and perhaps without realising, had let them colour my attitude to God. Unlike my mother, I was not consciously searching. Religion for me was merely an academic question. The God I believed in was a great universal force for good, given different names by different races, the Old Testament was the history of the Jewish people, and the New Testament comprised the teachings of Jesus Christ, who had lived on earth as God in human form in order to show mankind the pattern for a good life. That was really the extent of my creed. My Bible knowledge was scanty, I had no real conception of what it meant that Jesus died for our sins, and the Book of Revelation was simply a mystical fantasy. I was much intrigued by my mother's searchings and, I suppose, rather admiring of the way she seemed to have arrived at a personal truth. This truth, however, incorporated not one single aspect of the Christian faith. She detested what she called 'Churchianity' and held that all the miseries, wars and sufferings in history had been caused in the name of the Christian God. The name of Jesus was virtually unmentionable in her presence and I have seen her coming close to spitting in disdain if she heard it spoken.

These long conversations which we shared were a great trial for Sally for whom Christianity was a living reality. She had been educated at a Convent, but had not been confirmed and had quite independently discovered the truths of the Christian faith, initially from a book she had

had as a child called 'The Precious Gift' and subsequently through prayer and study of the Gospels. To sit and listen to me and my mother indulging in rambling, semi-intellectual discussions of much that was contrary to Christ's teachings caused her a great deal of distress, although I remained in blissful ignorance of this at the time.

On August 10th we were married at St Mary's Church, Henley-on-Thames according to the rites of the Anglican Church. I was happy enough to agree to a church wedding, both at Sally's request, and also because I knew I would actually enjoy the ritual of a formal ceremony, made more colourful by the military presence. We had the customary guard-of-honour of brother-officers from a variety of regiments, including a magnificently kilted Highlander. My own dress-uniform had needed the urgent attentions of a London tailor, as my lazy lifestyle, coupled with home cooking had not only restored my lost weight, but had added a noticeable surplus!

My mother, gratified by the splendour of it all, managed to endure, if not enjoy, the marriage service with its repeated references to God and Jesus Christ. Even up until the day before she had tried her best to persuade me against marriage, but in the end, there she was, resplendent in blue with the appropriate enormous hat, successfully giving the impression of docile concurrence with every word.

As for me, I thought I was taking the whole thing in my stride. I had not entered church for a long, long time, but the atmosphere, so well remembered from schooldays, was comfortably familiar and I felt quite at ease. It was only at the moment of making my vows that I became suddenly aware of the seriousness of what I was doing; I was making solemn promises, publicly, in the name of a God in whom I, in my own way, really did believe. It wasn't that I had any qualms about what I was promising;

I was totally certain that marriage to Sally was what I wanted more than anything in the world, but until that moment the spiritual dimension had had no significance for me. As we emerged into the brilliant sunshine of what was almost the only fine day in an appalling summer, the gravity which had come over me was quickly dispersed by the laughter and merriment which always follows the dignified formality of the wedding ceremony, and I put God back into the neat little compartment which I had made for him in my mind.

We were to stay at Sally's mother's home for the rest of my leave. I had to attend a month's training course in Wiltshire in September and was due to return to the Battalion in October, a prospect which began to seem less and less attractive the nearer it loomed. I was enjoying the freedom of life in Britain much more than I had anticipated. Having gone straight from the restrictions of public school into those of the army, it was exhilarating to be, for the first time in my life, free of all restraint. Did I, I began to wonder seriously, now want to give it up and resume the disciplined life of a soldier?

Sally was quite happy for me to continue with my military career and was looking forward to seeing Hong Kong, but she understood my misgivings and also the fact that there were other factors which I had to take into consideration. Although my mother had made a good recovery from her heart attack, her health was far from robust and she was now almost alone in England. My younger sister, Isobel, had joined the QARANCS (Queen Alexandra's Royal Army Nursing Corps) and was stationed in Aldershot, not too far distant from home, but both my brothers were by then serving overseas so I, as the eldest son, consequently felt a great deal of responsibility for my mother's welfare.

All in all, it was time to take stock of my life and make some decisions. I have described in an earlier chapter how

I joined the army more by chance than any planned intent; the time had now come for more careful thought, especially since having rather unexpectedly acquired a wife, I now had more than just myself to consider. I had reached the rank of captain, but I cannot honestly say that I regarded myself as a success in my chosen profession. Perhaps it was the rigorous discipline, or perhaps a rebellious side of my nature which I hadn't previously been conscious of, but whatever the reasons, my years in the Far East had been punctuated with regular skirmishes with authority. Looking back, it seemed to me that I was either the blue-eyed boy or else I was on the carpet. Did I have the necessary temperament, I wondered, to go further in the army? I knew that I would have to study fairly hard for entry to Staff College, and that even if I passed the exam there were no guarantees of a place because of the cut-backs being made at the time.

Sally and I had many lengthy discussions about our future. She had many friends in and around Henley who were involved in one way or another in the City, and when we all got together, usually in one of the local pubs, there was always a bit of talking shop, and I began to wonder whether I would find the life of a London businessman more satisfying than a career with the Gurkhas. Sally's mother was aware of my unsettled state of mind and, perhaps motivated by the chance of keeping her only daughter at home in England, tentatively mentioned a contact in the City, in fact a friend's nephew, who was chairman of a firm of Lloyd's brokers.

'Why not have a chat with him?' she suggested. 'It can't do any harm and you may find it interesting.'

The outcome was that I received a letter inviting me to meet this gentleman, and, during a very interesting interview, I finally made up my mind what I wanted to do. I explained that I would have to return to my regiment in order to resign my commission and go through the necessary formalities, and it was eventually agreed that the following spring, I would join their company and begin a new career.

Meanwhile I was still a serving officer in Her Majesty's Armed Forces, and when the long period of leave finally reached its end, Sally and I made preparations for the journey to Hong Kong.

That eighteen-hour flight back to the colony was unquestionably the worst air-trip I have ever made or wish to make. From the Persian Gulf to Singapore we flew into incredible storms and, try as he would, the pilot of our RAF VC10 could not avoid them. We would climb and climb in an attempt to leave the bad weather below us, then each time encounter an air pocket and suddenly drop several hundred feet. All of us on board were service personnel and the crew had their hands full for the entire flight, calming frightened children (and terrified adults!) while trying to serve such meals and drinks as were needed. Not many of us felt much like eating on that nightmare journey and when we touched down in Singapore the more severe cases of shock were immediately transported by the waiting ambulances to hospital to recover.

When we finally disembarked in Hong Kong the sense of relief was indescribable and I was thankful for the two or three days which I was allowed for re-orientation before reporting back. When I did, it was to a new Commanding Officer who had joined us from the Seventh Gurkhas. After the exchange of formalities Colonel John Whitehead outlined his plans for my coming tour of duty, which included my taking command of B-Company, and I listened, rather nervously, knowing what had to be said. When he finished speaking, I took a deep breath and told him of my wish to resign.

He listened carefully and with great courtesy to my

explanation of my mother's situation and my reservations about Staff College, and, after reassuring himself that I had given the matter proper consideration, agreed to put the necessary wheels in motion for me to leave the regiment the following spring. In the meantime, I was to take over B-Company as arranged.

While we looked for our own accommodation, Sally and I stayed with a brother-officer and his wife, a couple who had been married in England just a short time before us. Married quarters were notoriously difficult to come by so we eventually rented a private house in the New Territories, near the border with China. It was owned by a European who had a Chinese wife, and it was situated less than a mile from the border crossing. Across the garden was a little shanty village and from there came a permanent background noise of the click of Mah-Jong tiles, as the older inhabitants whiled away the hours.

Ahead of us was an eight-week separation while I did a tour of duty in Malaya. Fortunately Sally found a post as secretary to the Secretary of the Royal Hong Kong Golf Club, so I was able to leave with the knowledge that she would not find time hanging too heavily on her hands during my absence.

I spent my time in Malaya updating and maintaining our existing jungle-warfare skills, as well as trying to impart some of them to the regiment's new recruits. It was a great pleasure to me to renew my acquaintance with former friends and Gurkha Officers who had known me as a raw Second Lieutenant. The Second Lieutenant now under my command reminded me very much of myself in the early days. We shared the same independent turn of mind and generally got on very well. This happy professional relationship helped to make service life more enjoyable for me than it had previously been and I couldn't help wondering whether, if my first six years in the regiment had been more like the last three, I would have come to the decision to leave the army.

However, that decision had been made, and acted upon. In February Sally flew back to England, and, two months later, I said goodbye for the last time to my regiment and, with very mixed emotions, embarked on the long journey home.

4

Climbing the Ladder

We set up home in Surrey. Sally took a job with a local firm of solicitors and I joined the army of commuters on the 8.15 to Waterloo. Having been away from England for so long it was hardly surprising that at first I should find everything a great novelty and in its own way quite exciting. Any forays I had formerly made into London during my time at Sandhurst and later whilst on leave, had been confined to the West End, and the square mile of the capital known as the City was for the most part a complete mystery to me. I caused considerable amusement when, given my first errand in my new job, I had to ask where to find the Bank of England! Some of the younger clerical workers, East Enders all, took me under their wing after the initial period of good-natured mockery, and educated me in the geography of their native terrain. Not surprisingly, the local pubs were the main points of reference and I very soon discovered where to go for the best beer and sandwiches.

I found I was enjoying civilian life very much but one aspect of it began to cause concern—finance. Even with Sally's earnings, we were struggling to save for a house of our own.

At my initial interview I had been warned that I would

have to start at the bottom and that, as most of my contemporaries had come into the profession direct from school or University, I would find myself, at the age of twenty-eight, something of an old man to be learning the job from square one. I had been prepared for this and was enjoying find out about the intricacies of City business, but money, or the shortage of it, began to assume a larger and larger role in my life. When my mother, during a visit to us, suggested that I have my horoscope cast, I must say that my reasons for agreeing were mostly materialistic. I wanted very much to be promised great financial prosperity. As it turned out, the three-year forecast was disappointingly bland, full of wide generalisations, as I suspect many of them are, and as far as I was concerned, a total waste of my time and money.

My mother was by then very much taken up with the Aquarian Gospel. Rosicrucianism had come under her scrutiny and she had dabbled in that for quite some time before moving on in her search. She now carried on her lengthy discussions with my brother John who had recently left the army and, as I had done, was staying with mother prior to his marriage. John, too, was searching for something and at that time was finding his personal answer in Theosophy. I remained, as before, slightly detached, interested in discussion only for its own sake. I was searching for something entirely different—financial success. The Bible says that one cannot serve God and mammon, and, during this period of my life, I was far too occupied serving mammon to worry about God.

It was daily becoming clearer to me that I could not afford to remain in my present situation. The novelty of London was wearing off, and I was beginning to wonder whether I might have made a terrible mistake in leaving the army. It was not yet nine months since I had resigned my commission so, had I then decided to resume my military career, I could have done so without loss of rank.

Sally and I agonised over our future; she was happy to back me whichever way I chose to go, but I eventually decided that I had not had enough time in the City to make a balanced judgement and therefore I would carry on. I had become very interested in the broking side of my job and was keen to become directly involved, so I approached an employment agency which specialised in the field of insurance, and through them I was able to find a position in which I could develop this interest. An added attraction was the prospect of some foreign travel, particularly to the Far East, and thinking about that, I was surprised to realise how much I missed that part of the world which had been my home for a large proportion of my life.

The four years which I spent with that company as assistant to one of the partners were a very satisfying and profitable time for me, thanks largely to the excellent relationship which developed between me and my immediate boss, Bernard Wilsher. I had to accompany him on his annual trip to Japan and the better I got to know him, the more I came to like and respect him. After a day's business which was nearly always followed by dinner with our hosts, Bernard and I would adjourn to the hotel bar and relax over a drink or two while we discussed the day's events and chatted generally. Bernard not only taught me much of what he knew about the world of reinsurance, gained from thirty years in the profession, but he was also happy to satisfy, as far as he was able, my great curiosity about Japan and its people.

I was captivated and intrigued by the Japanese. As honoured guests we were treated with the utmost kindness and courtesy; nothing was too much trouble for our hosts. Away from the teeming city streets I marvelled at the exquisite tranquillity of the gardens in the old capital, Kyoto, and at the magnificent artistry evident in the temples and shrines. Here was peace, order and perfect harmony, together with a sense of timelessness which made it difficult to realise that only a few miles away, a technological and economic revolution was taking place.

Based as it was on Emperor-worship and Shintoism, Japanese society appeared to be rigidly structured in a way that was almost feudalistic. Everyone knew his place in the hierarchy and was expected to behave accordingly. In the world of business there was a rigid protocol to be observed, and woe betide any aspiring young executive if he failed to do so.

This was my first encounter with Shintoism as a national religion, and I found nothing in its system to recommend it. It was one of the many subjects which Bernard and I used to discuss during our late night sessions in the bar. Bernard was a professed atheist yet rarely have I met a man who displayed more of the Christian ethic in his everyday life. In many ways he reminded me of my old schoolmasters, George Ullyott and Richard Fletcher; he was invariably courteous to all, and in his business dealings showed the highest integrity. A man of considerable intellect, he had one of the most logical, analytical minds I have ever come across and this rather cerebral approach to life allowed of no spiritual dimension. He was immensely liberal in his attitude to others' beliefs, recognising that for many people faith of some kind was a very necessary part of their existence, but it was not something which he himself needed, and furthermore he would have considered it the height of bad manners to try to interfere with or to influence anyone's private beliefs in any way. The fact that he believed that there was nothing at all after death did not prevent him from leading an exemplary life, and he remains in my memory as one of the most admirable of men.

Towards the end of 1973 Bernard let me know that the company was to be involved in a merger, which would almost certainly mean changes for both of us, so I decided that it was time to move on. The experience of the last four years stood me in good stead and I was asked by the managing director of a large Lloyd's Broking House to take over from him the Japanese and Asian business, to develop and service it and at the same time to open up new markets in Communist Europe. It was an exciting challenge and one I welcomed. Thanks to my former boss I had managed to acquire some expertise in the world of reinsurance, I was daily acquiring more and I began to feel that at last I was starting the climb to the top, which is where I intended to be. Sally and I were now a family, Edward having arrived in February 1971 and Louise in the December of the following year. We had bought a comfortable family house in Wokingham, Berkshire, and were at last beginning to enjoy a measure of, if not exactly affluence, at least freedom from financial worries.

In my new job I found myself for the first time working in Lloyd's Old Building and enjoying the social contact with fellow-commuters and old friends from Henley. It was here, over coffee, that I was introduced to Hamish Morrison. For the life of me I can't recall exactly how and when the subject of Freemasonry first came into our chats, but when I heard it mentioned in our usual group in the Coffee Room, I expressed an interest and mentioned that my grandfather had been a member of that organisation. A week later Hamish invited me to lunch in the Captain's Room, told me that he and several others in the group were Freemasons and asked me if I was interested in joining them. I accepted with alacrity, thus setting in motion the wheels which were to lead to my initiation into the Craft.

If my wife were asked what she remembers most about the year 1974 she might well say that it was the remarkably little time she and I spent together. We moved into our new house in Wokingham in February and, as is often the case, Sally was the one who had the job of turning it into a home, making new friends and generally sorting things out, while coping with two small children. Back in the Thames Valley we were on reasonably familiar territory, not too far from Sally's mother's home, so she was at least able to renew contact with old friends and not have to start completely from scratch in making some kind of social life which would help life to be a little more tolerable in my long absences.

I tackled my new job with enthusiasm, not least because of the prospect of my first ever trip behind the Iron Curtain. In May, shortly after my initiation into Freemasonry, I left for Prague. I was very curious to see life in a Communist state at first hand but my anticipation was tempered somewhat by the memory of a story which Bernard had recounted on one of our trips to Japan. He himself had had dealings with the State Insurance Company of Czechoslovakia and on one occasion had entertained its Reinsurance Manager and his deputy to dinner, during which the Manager chatted away in a very relaxed fashion and at one point, indulged in a little mild criticism of his country's political regime. The deputy, in contrast, spoke hardly at all throughout the course of the evening but listened with close attention to the conversation around him. Shortly after this trip the letters Bernard received from the Company, which customarily bore the Manager's signature, began to arrive signed, not by him, but by the former deputy. On inquiring, the London Market was informed that this particular manager was no longer an employee of the State Insurance Company. Speculation as to what sinister fate had overtaken the unfortunate man knew no bounds, and when I arrived at the Company's offices on my first trip to Prague, I looked into the expressionless eyes of the new manager, and I wondered.

The severe political regime did not prevent me from enjoying my first visit to Czechoslovakia. Prague is a beautiful city and I was lucky enough to meet another

English businessman in my hotel, so together we explored its streets and sampled the numerous beer cellars. Anyone who saw the film *Amadeus* will recall that much of it was filmed in Prague, due to the fact that the city has not suffered too much from what town-planners call modernisation, which is usually a euphemism for the most philistine acts of destruction carried out in the name of progress in many European cities. Wenceslas Square was an absolute delight, and the warren of narrow streets totally fascinating to me.

Much as I enjoyed the aesthetic pleasures of Prague, it was nevertheless something of a relief to fly on to Budapest, and here I found a very different atmosphere. I was beginning to appreciate the error of mentally classing all members of the Eastern bloc together into one category. I discovered that they were as distinctive from one another as the countries of the West, and even under a Moscow-influenced system, national characteristics showed through. The Hungarian people gave little indication of being oppressed, and life in general in Budapest seemed much more carefree than in Prague. There were a lot more smiles and laughter in evidence everywhere, and when I entered the hotel dining-room and heard the strains of the three-piece orchestra, I felt just as though I had strayed onto a film set of the pre-war years.

I would have loved more time to sample the local restaurants, where I could perhaps have heard the authentic gypsy musicians playing, but I had a strict itinerary to follow, and as soon as my business was concluded, I reluctantly left the bustling, friendly city on the shores of the not-so-blue Danube, and flew on to Sofia, the capital of Bulgaria.

If I had thought the Czech regime oppressive, I soon began to feel that compared with Bulgaria, it was almost liberal. Without exaggeration, Bulgaria frightened me, so tangible was the oppression under which life there operated. I had not realised quite how much the State Police were involved in everyday business and was dismayed and depressed by something which occurred at my first business lunch. I was being entertained by two gentlemen from the company I was visiting, and was trying to conduct the type of social chat which is usual on these occasions. I couldn't help noticing that one of my two companions seemed very ill at ease; he sat nervously on the edge of his chair, and before making any response to my small talk, would glance quickly at his colleague and away again in a way which I found a little disconcerting. Memories of Bernard's experience flashed into my mind, but I was still taken aback when this man seized the opportunity of a moment on our own to beg me not to put any personal questions to him. My expression must have shown the surprise I felt at this reaction to my 'harmless' conversation, so he hurriedly informed me that he was not a party member, and he did not want to risk saying anything that might compromise him in front of his colleague, who was.

The man's discomfiture throughout the course of the meal was quite pitiable. The other was obviously well aware of it, and in fact seemed to be deriving a warped enjoyment from the situation. For my part, I made sure that the conversation from then on remained strictly on business lines or such non-controversial topics as the weather of our respective countries.

It was beginning to dawn on me just how fortunate I was to be living in the West, in a democracy. Never, I felt, had Winston Churchill spoken a truer word than when he observed that though democracy was a very bad form of government, all the others were so much worse. I thought of the many political and religious discussions I'd taken part in with all types of people and with great enjoyment, able to speak my mind quite freely with no fear of repercussions; of the satirising and lampooning of politicians which the Western media love to indulge in; of Hyde Park Corner where any Tom, Dick or Harry, of sound mind or otherwise, can get up on his hind legs and harangue the powers that be to his heart's content, while the worst discipline facing him would be a polite 'Would you mind moving along, Sir?' from an urbane London bobby.

Bucharest, my next port of call, came as a blessed relief. Here there was virtually no evidence at all of any repression, and though I later learned that the regime was in fact quite Stalinesque in its brutality, that was far from obvious to the casual visitor like myself, and I spent a very happy few days there.

My fondest memories of my time in Eastern Europe, however, are of Yugoslavia. Here, as I was constantly reminded, the system is socialist, not communist, and my business contacts took pains to explain to me how that worked in practice, with worker-participation, promotion through merit even as far as Board level, and so forth. Despite all this, I can't say that I found them any easier to deal with than some of the other nationalities!

After a day's business business I found myself alone in my hotel room. It was one of those soft evenings in spring which really seem to be promising summer, and I felt restless, so I set off to explore Belgrade. As in Hungary there was a carefree atmosphere in the streets. Tourism was beginning to make its mark in Yugoslavia and the capital's hotels and restaurants were all busy putting on their summer facades ready for visitors. I wandered about wherever the fancy took me and after an hour or so found myself in a little side street, delightfully picturesque with its cobbles and gabled buildings. On the corner was a small cafe, just like the ones which abound in Paris, with tables outside on the pavement and music coming from somewhere within. I found a seat and ordered a beer.

'Ah!' exclaimed the waiter who took my order. 'You are British!'

He seemed quite pleased at his discovery so I felt free to admit to my nationality, and he disappeared to bring my drink, smiling broadly as he went. Inside the cafe I could see a group of men sitting around a corner table, all laughing and talking noisily. When the waiter returned with my beer, two of the group came with him, smiling and nodding in the friendliest way. They seated themselves at my table and began a conversation in reasonably good English, during which they established that I was a businessman on my first trip to their country and that I had formerly served in the British Army. They seemed a little disappointed on learning that I hadn't served in the World War Two but, undeterred, they carried on the conversation with great energy and gradually the others moved across to join us.

They were all obviously older than I, perhaps in their sixties, and it soon transpired that they had been with the partisans during the Second World War, and were anxious to know if I was personally acquainted with Brigadier Fitzroy McLean who had acted as liaison between them and the British Government during the Nazi occupation of Yugoslavia. Hiding my wounded vanity—did I look as old as that? I really must have a word with Sally about my appearance—I regretted that I could not claim the Brigadier's acquaintance, but happily they did not let that prevent them from making me one of their party and a very drunken evening followed.

We drank toast after toast—to Fitzroy McLean, to the British Army, to Queen Elizabeth, Winston Churchill, Marshall Tito and innumerable others whose names became less and less discernible as bottle after bottle of the local fire-water appeared, was emptied, removed and replaced. I had had a thorough grounding in the serious consumption of alcohol during my time with the Gurkhas, nevertheless I found by the small hours of the morning the picturesque streets of Belgrade had somehow all begun to look exactly alike, and rather blurred at that; so I was very happy to be helped into a taxi and driven back to the hotel, after many fond farewells and expressions of undying esteem from the exuberant and gregarious Yugoslavs.

During my flight home from that first European trip, I reflected on the great difference in the style of doing business between the countries I had just left, and Japan, which I had come to know so well in my previous job. In Japan, the ultimate exponent of capitalism, I was shown quite overwhelming kindness and entertained with lavish hospitality by my business associates, in total contrast to the stiff, formal courtesy of their Communist counterparts. I smiled to myself as I recalled my return from my first Tokyo visit; then I was bearing several beautiful pearl brooches and an elegant leather handbag for Sally, generous gifts from my hosts, which I gathered was quite customary for first-time visitors. I hoped she would be just as pleased with my present humble offering of a bottle of duty-free perfume.

I was looking forward to returning to Japan very soon as part of a seven-week trip I was due to make to the Far East, which would also include Korea, Hong Kong, Manila, Singapore, Kuala Lumpur, Djakarta and Bangkok. When I did return, however, full of enthusiasm and anxious to renew old acquaintances, I was rather unexpectedly made aware of another very great difference between us in our attitude to work.

Because I was the first representative of my present company to visit Tokyo, I called on all the insurance companies there, including those I had visited in earlier years, but any expectations I might have had regarding preferential treatment for an old friend were soon dashed. I was received with the customary courtesy but it was made very clear to me that I must take my chances, as it were, with my business competitors, and not presume on old acquaintances. I was a little disconcerted by this treatment and then I recalled something of what Bernard Wilsher had told me about the Japanese attitude to employment. I realised that, in their eyes, I had committed an act of betrayal in leaving one company to go to another. In Japan the way to the top is by staying with one firm and earning promotion gradually; the western practice of furthering one's career by moving from employer to employer is quite alien to them, and by doing so, I was diminished in their eyes. Fortunately, I was still representing a large company and they were pragmatic enough to see the benefit to themselves of continuing to deal with me, so I was happy to return home with a significant piece of business and to have learned an interesting lesson in the process.

My travels came to an abrupt end in Djakarta when I received a rather desperate call from Sally. Our son, Edward, who was by then three-and-a-half, had seen so little of me that he had become convinced I had gone away for ever and was consequently in a state of some distress. Nothing Sally or anyone else could say would comfort or reassure him, so Sally had had to resort to putting through a call to Indonesia to ask me to speak to Edward myself.

My boss had joined me in Djakarta, bringing his wife with him. She was a very understanding and caring woman and was quite horrified when I told her the reason behind Sally's call. She was very much aware of the problems faced by young families with absentee fathers, and being a woman of strong character, she had no compunction in making her views known to her husband.

'Ian must go home,' she concluded. 'Now!' Such was the strength of her personality, and, of course, the sympathetic nature of her husband, that within seventy-two hours of Sally's call, I was safely back in the bosom of my family.

5

A Realisation of Ambitions

I did not share the Japanese attitude to career building, and while I like to think that I always behaved ethically, I had learned to have no compunction in changing my situation to further my own prospects. I had very quickly realised that the real money was to be made only at the top, that is, at director level, and I intended to get to that level as quickly as I could, especially since I had made a late start in the City. When I realised that a very determined power struggle was going on within the company, I decided to opt out. I had no taste for office politics and had not been long enough in the job to make any balanced decisions, so, finding myself somewhat caught between two factions, it seemed to me prudent to withdraw.

It happened that I was approached by a friend in the Aviation Company of our group who was about to start up his own company, with outside financial backing, and together we began operating as a small insurance production house, under the umbrella of three larger broking houses. It was not long before I began to question the wisdom of this move. The company was strongly aviation orientated and I found that there was no natural outlet for my own particular expertise. I really needed to create my own niche, my own area of operating, and in my determination to secure my position, I began to dabble in ventures which were outside the field of insurance.

By this time I had formed many contacts in London and throughout Europe and the Far East, and I was able to make some useful introductions, always keeping my eyes and ears open for the chance of a good investment. One day, in the late summer of 1975, I was introduced to a personable young man who worked as an investment consultant and gave every impression of being very successful in his field. He spoke knowledgeably on the City and industry, and I mentally labelled him a useful person to know. When he telephoned me several days later and suggested a meeting, I was quite ready to listen to what he might have to say. His proposals certainly appeared very attractive and I was eager to discuss them with my partner and our parent company. I was anxious at this point in my new job to establish myself firmly, and I now saw the possibility of doing so, by means of concluding a satisfactory deal with my new contact.

Losing no time, I relayed all the information I'd gathered from him to the Board of our parent company, and was delighted when Simon, the Managing Director, agreed to set up a meeting with this young Mr Andrews, who had so impressed me.

I entered the boardroom on the appointed day, feeling rather pleased with myself and looking forward to seeing the first of many lucrative contracts being drawn up. Andrews arrived and I introduced him to the Board. Simon greeted the newcomer with his usual courtesy and invited him to sit down. He then produced a large dossier which he opened on the desk in front of him and with one hand on this, he addressed the young man sitting expectantly opposite him.

'Mr Andrews,' Simon began, 'before we embark on our discussions I feel it only fair to advise you of something rather worrying which has been going on in London recently, and which has been drawn to my attention. It appears that there is a quite unscrupulous trickster operating in the Markets at present, and what is more, he is using your name in defrauding companies such as ourselves of rather substantial amounts of money.'

I sat up in astonishment at this disclosure, and that astonishment grew as Simon went on to recount a long list of this scoundrel's misdeeds, which seemed to cover everything from juvenile crime, resulting in a stay in Borstal, to wife-beating, on which charge criminal proceedings were pending. His speciality seemed to be financial dealings across a wide spectrum, all of a dubious nature.

Simon finished the catalogue of crime and sat back in his chair. He smiled gently at Andrews.

'I thought that this was something you really ought to be aware of prior to any discussions you might want to have with me and my Board of Directors.'

I looked at Andrews, who had half risen from his seat and was attempting to gather up his papers and briefcase. His face was ashen and he was muttering something about arranging another meeting after he'd looked into what he'd just heard. I still did not understand what was going on and I saw him out of the building in something of a state of bewilderment, promising that I would be in touch. Andrews, I noted with some concern, looked quite ill and I was sorry for the shock Simon's news must have given him.

I hurried back to the boardroom, anxious for an explanation and not a little peeved at the turn events had taken. To my horror, I learned from Simon that my competent young businessman was in fact the front man for a very successful international confidence trickster. More by good luck than anything, he had managed to keep one step ahead of the law while setting up fraudulent deals with gullible idiots like myself. When the victim was nicely hooked, the big man would move in and land the catch.

When I had first mentioned Andrews to Simon, that very astute and careful man had made discreet inquiries which had revealed just what kind of a contact I had made! In my eagerness to pull off a good deal quickly, I could have had my fingers very badly burned; it was only thanks to Simon that I had not suffered a major professional setback, and in the process ended up looking very foolish indeed. I was furious with myself, and grateful for the tolerance and understanding of most of my colleagues, most especially to Simon himself who had taught me in no uncertain way that I had to learn, as he put it, the difference between need and greed.

Unfortunately not all my colleagues were as understanding as Simon had been over this incident and it soon became apparent that there really was no role for me in the future of the company. I was sorry that the parting was not as amicable as it might have been, but I realised that I had been in the wrong situation and that I needed to get back into the place where I felt on safe ground, in business that I knew well. Ironically my efforts in the company, prior to the Andrews debacle, culminated after my departure, in one of the Lloyd's Broking houses for whom we were doing business, capturing the insurance account of a major Far Eastern airline. The words of one of the directors when he gave me this welcome news were something of a solace to my battered pride.

'That was a fine piece of business you got for us, Ian,' he said, 'and just remember, no one can ever take that achievement from you.'

My real expertise lay in my knowledge of the Far East and towards the end of 1975 I accepted a job as consultant specialising in Far Eastern affairs with a Lloyd's broking company. I was glad to be back on familiar territory. I had come to the conclusion that my particular professional niche would be as a director of a small subsidiary company within a group. I felt, from my experience, that that was where I could function best, and that the position would give me the authority I wanted, as well as providing the financial rewards I was seeking. When, just over a year later, I was invited onto the Board of the international subsidiary of the company, I felt that I had found my niche at last.

So began another happy episode in my business life, bringing the same sort of fulfilment and satisfaction that I had enjoyed in my four years under Bernard Wilsher. I had wide responsibilities, I was directly involved in broking, and my self-confidence was slowly being restored after the severe knock it had received in my last venture.

It was during this time that I really began to understand the workings of the City at grass roots level, and I found that the more I saw, the less I liked. The situation was very much one of dog eat dog; cliques abounded and factions were formed, which usually resulted in someone being sacrificed on the altar of self-interest. I found internal office politics the hardest of all to deal with, and was always the last to learn of anything that was happening behind the scenes. I had been a director for about two-and-a-half years when I began to be seriously irritated by the situation which I saw in the company. I was annoyed by what I considered to be poor administration and frustrated by a policy which precluded me from instigating the changes which I felt to be essential in the light of my foreign experiences. The niche which I had thought ideal was becoming too restricted, and I mentioned this to a friend in the Market on a day when I was feeling a little more frustrated than usual. I was not prepared at all for his response, which was to suggest starting up on my own. This was a possibility which had not occurred to me before, but when this friend mentioned that his boss would quite likely be interested in backing me, I began to warm to the idea.

Things happened very rapidly after that, and in September 1979 I launched my own company with a total staff of two, that is myself and a secretary. I was well pleased with life in general at this point, and myself in particular. I was now my own boss, with my own company to run as I chose, albeit only as a 30% shareholder, and the world was my oyster. I was not yet forty, and the future was looking brighter by the minute.

From the outset I had very definite ideas on how I was going to run my company. My nine years in the City had taught me a lot about finance but I knew there were certain areas where I was still weak. I had made a lot of mistakes and I spent a considerable amount of time examining and analysing what had happened in my previous jobs. One of the conclusions I came to was that I had not always shown the right approach in dealing with immediate colleagues and I realised that my military background was more than likely the culprit here. The direct approach of a soldier, to which I was accustomed, was not ideal for life in the City where tact and diplomacy, superfluous qualities in the Brigade of Gurkhas, were the order of the day.

There were several other areas in which, on looking back, I could have acted differently. There are, after all, ways of telling a man he is wrong, and of making suggestions, however certain you might be of your own rightness. One aspect of business life, though, I was determined I would never condone, and that was the ruthless, self-seeking attitude which led to clandestine meetings and underhand dealings which left one not knowing where one stood. I was as ambitious as the next man but I could honestly say that my ambition had been overt and I had conducted all my dealings quite openly. I might have been too naïve in taking people at their face value, as my near-miss with the con-man illustrated, but, although I had learned a hard lesson there, I did not intend to let it alter the way I dealt with colleagues. I was prepared to be taken at my face value, and to let all those with whom I had dealings know that they could rely on me to be completely straightforward.

I had now been a Freemason for five years and as I progressed through the Craft I had become more and more conscious of the standards which all members were constrained to live by. At my initiation the Worshipful Master had delivered the customary charge to the Entered Apprentice, in which great stress is laid upon the individual's conduct. I was instructed to regard the Bible, or the Volume of the Sacred Law as it was termed, as 'the unerring standard of truth and justice', and to 'regulate (my) actions by the divine precepts it contains.' In fact the early part of that charge basically comprises the Golden Rule, that we should put God first and always do to our neighbour as we would have him do to us.

The working tools which I was given at the following meeting, when I passed to the Second Degree of Freemasonry, were a square, a level and a plumb-rule, and I was advised that these instruments taught respectively, morality, equality and justice and uprightness of life and actions. Each subsequent meeting I attended, when I heard the various addresses, charges and explanations, all confirmed the initial belief which I had had in the innate goodness of the Craft, and the integrity of its members. I had learned that fellow-masons could be depended upon, that they were not party to the dog eat dog struggle which I so disliked. I was always very conscious that I must not use Freemasonry for business reasons and so I tried to keep the two spheres strictly segregated, not the easiest thing in the world, particularly when one needed to know who was totally dependable and who was not.

As I became more and more impressed with Freemasonry so my disenchantment with the Church increased. Sally worshipped regularly at our local parish church, and I usually went along, more to please her than anything else, but it all seemed just as hollow and meaningless as it had done in my schooldays. I began to understand what my mother had meant by the scathing term 'Churchianity', when I contrasted the attitudes of devout piety which I saw in the congregation each Sunday, with the behaviour I witnessed during the rest of the week, often in the City amongst men in the same profession as myself.

I also compared the two rituals, of the Anglican church and the Craft, and found that of the Craft infinitely superior. To me, Freemasonry was firmly rooted in Bible history and all its rites and practices reflected this. It was taken very seriously by its members, and every man who had a part to play in a meeting would spend a lot of time learning that part thoroughly. Not for them the facile reading from liturgy which I sat through each Sunday. I would watch the Anglican priests as they intoned the service and feel that in Freemasonry I had access to deeper scriptural truths which even they did not know. It had been hinted to me several times that the real secrets of the Craft were accessible only at the higher levels and I was looking forward to discovering them. There is a natural progression through the 'ranks' of Freemasonry until one becomes Master of a Lodge, and I had gathered that when I reached that office, many more of the Craft's secrets would be revealed to me. I had no idea what these might comprise but from what I had learned thus far, I felt sure that everything would be solidly based on the Bible, and I looked forward to finding them out. Meanwhile, I wallowed in a feeling of smug superiority to the professed Christians with whom I met together each Sunday in church.

It was only when we moved house and therefore changed our place of worship that this attitude of mine began to soften. The Thames Valley atmosphere became intolerable for Sally who was permanently prey to attacks of bronchitis, and when the children began to be affected as well, we decided that enough was enough and set out to look for higher ground. East of London seemed sensible for commuting into the City and we eventually fixed on Crowborough in East Sussex. We moved in in April 1978, just a few days after the birth of our third child, William, and in time began to attend All Saints, the Anglican parish church.

The first time I went to a service there, rather reluctantly as always, I sensed something different. The whole proceedings seemed somehow more alive, the members of the congregation appeared to be really sharing in the service, instead of having merely passive roles, and the vicar himself actually looked as though he believed absolutely in every word he spoke.

Thereafter my church attendances were not quite so grudging and I even began to enjoy some of the services. When the time came for William to be christened, my complacency received something of a shock, for I discovered that this vicar was not prepared to baptise a child simply at the parents' request, but wanted to establish first that they understood fully the implications of the ceremony, and that they were themselves committed Christians. To this end Sally and I were 'interviewed' at length and I discovered, much to my chagrin, that it was not enough that I, rather condescendingly, attended church on Sundays; my beliefs were put under scrutiny, and here the problem arose.

Although, through my attendance at Lodge meetings, my concepts of God and Jesus Christ were crystallising, I still incorporated many of the ideas which I had found in Eastern religions, the major one of these being the doctrine of reincarnation, and after much discussion it looked as if the Anglican priest of our new parish was going to find himself unable to baptise my son. Finally it was because of Sally that he agreed to do so. Sally's adherence to the Christian faith was total and overt. It was our assurance that William would be taught the tenets of this faith as his older brother and sister had been, which persuaded the vicar that baptism would be in order.

Uncomfortable though this interview had been, it shook me out of my complacency and my respect for my new parish priest increased because of it. During our time as members of his church the Christian and the Masonic ideals began, without my realising it, to merge in my mind. Previously the two had run along diverging tracks and I had compartmentalised them, never believing that the twain could ever meet. Now, however, I recognised the similarity between the standards of conduct which were impressed on us at Lodge meetings, and the teachings of Jesus Christ. Together they seemed to make an ideal pattern for life, and when I began my own company in 1979, I determined to run it on Christo-Masonic principles, as I saw them.

By that time we had left Crowborough and All Saints, and moved six miles or so to one of Sussex's most picturesque villages, Mayfield, the seat of the very early Archbishops of Canterbury, including Saint Dunstan, to whom the parish church was dedicated.

A year in Crowborough had convinced us that the south-east was the right area for us, and we looked round for a suitable house in which we could settle. I suppose that I was the real instigator of this move; I had very definite ideas on what I wanted to achieve in my domestic life, just as I had in business, and, of course, the two were linked. What I wanted to provide for my family was a large house in the country, adequate means to enjoy it, and a good education for my children. To be able to do all this, I needed the sort of income that I could only get from a position fairly near the top in the world of reinsurance, my world. Starting my own company meant that I was well on the way to realising my ambitions, and in the autumn of 1979 I had every reason to believe that the way ahead was clear. I had a beautiful converted oast house in a lovely part of the country, I had started my two older children at established prep schools, I was driving a Mercedes saloon and Sally a large Peugeot family estate car, we enjoyed a full and varied social life and I was enormously enjoying my masonic career. To all outward appearances, I had it made.

6

The Shadow of a Doubt

My first step in getting my newly formed company off the ground was to head out to my old haunts in the Far East. Armed with a large piece of reinsurance business given me by my financial backers I flew to Tokyo and approached my former business contacts. I explained that I was now operating on my own account and confidently awaited their pleased response. How misguided I was: I was now made to realise the full implications of the Japanese work ethic. As far as they were concerned, I was now quite beyond the pale. Leaving one company might be forgivable, understandable even, but to do what I had done was totally inexcusable. Doors which I had fondly hoped to find welcomingly open, or at least encouragingly ajar, were in fact very firmly closed, and I returned home empty-handed and had to content myself with placing some business with an American company in London.

I spent most of the next twelve months establishing contacts in London and generally making my existence and aims known in the London Market. By the spring of 1980 it had become obvious that I needed an accounts manager, and I took on Tom Harvey, a specialist in reinsurance accounting who had previously worked for my backing company. Tom was well-acquainted with the world of reinsurance so I felt quite confident of his abilities and very optimistic about our future prospects.

I was not even discouraged by a warning which he gave me soon after joining, that he was concerned about relations between our financial backers and their continental parent company. Tom felt that their present arrangement would only last for a few more years, five at most, but when he voiced his fears to me I saw no problem arising as I had already formed plans of my own to diversify somewhat and enter the area of direct insurance. Quite by chance, in fact through the man whose house I had bought, I had met a motor insurance broker who ran a very large organisation in the South of England. He had already placed some business in Lloyd's and was looking for an additional avenue, so I made inquiries and, on finding that his name was well respected in the City and that he was known for his integrity as well as his business acumen, I declared that this area, hitherto quite foreign to me, was certainly worth investigating. This I did, and we eventually came to an arrangement whereby my company would be directly involved in motor insurance from the following January.

From the beginning this new side of my business prospered and it soon became necessary for me to look for an additional manager who could handle the increasing work load and also implement the long-term strategy which I had worked out. I let it be known that I was looking for a good man and another provincial broker friend told me about Maurice Collighan. It appeared that Maurice had worked as a business producer in a Lloyd's broking house until illness had forced him to take a long period of absence, about six months in all. The company had held his job for him, but on his return he found that a junior colleague had been promoted over his head, and the resulting situation was extremely unsatisfactory. I was sympathetic to the man's plight and when I met him I was impressed by his obvious enthusiasm for his work. Furthermore, he was recommended by what I considered an exemplary source, so in June 1981 Maurice joined Tom Harvey and myself. The company was growing nicely.

From day one Maurice inspired confidence and I felt quite happy at leaving the new business in his hands while I myself concentrated on the original reinsurance side, the side I knew and understood. It was now necessary for me to go to America to service the business I had placed there with the London correspondents, so I arranged a trip for the autumn of that year and decided to go on to Australia to see if I could make some new contacts there. My brother, Graham, had settled in Melbourne so I telephoned him and arranged to see him on my visit. His reaction surprised me.

'I'm glad you're coming,' he said. 'I've been intending to get in touch with you for a while now. There's something I want to talk over with you, something that's worrying me a great deal.'

My first thought was of illness, that he or one of the family might have some serious complaint, but Graham assured me that they were all fit and well and that what he wanted to discuss with me was nothing domestic.

'What is it, then?' I demanded, a little impatiently. Graham, I thought, was being unnecessarily mysterious. His next words intrigued me even more.

'I can't really tell you much on the international phone,' he said, 'but there's something very strange going on in the world.'

I was about to make some flippant remark or other, but then I stopped. There was an unmistakable and unusual note of gravity in Graham's voice, which disturbed me.

'Are you sure you're all right, old man?' I asked him. 'I must say you don't sound quite yourself.'

'I'm fine,' he answered, 'but I am worried about something I've discovered, and I want to talk to someone about it.'

Graham's words were at the back of my mind all the time I was in America. I couldn't for the life of me think what it might be that was causing him such concern and I was quite anxious to get to Melbourne to talk to him. At San Francisco my flight was delayed for half-an-hour so I took the opportunity of browsing round the bookshop, something I always enjoyed. I set about looking for something interesting to help make the long haul across the Pacific more bearable and my attention was caught by a couple of paperbacks by an American author, Hal Lindsey. The name meant nothing to me, but I was immediately drawn to the subject of the books. They were entitled respectively *Satan is Alive and Well on Planet Earth* and *There's a New World Coming* and both dealt with biblical prophecy and its fulfilment. It was a subject in which I had become more and more interested in recent months as my attitudes to Christianity and the Bible were being slowly modified by my church-going and my membership of the Craft. The concept of the end times, that is the period which the Bible says leads up to the second coming of Christ, had begun to fascinate me. It appeared to me from everything I had read that all religions, Islam, Buddhists, Hindus, seemed to be expecting a 'coming' of some kind, and several other cults were proclaiming a forthcoming cataclysmic event of a similar nature.

I managed to read most of both books during the flight to Sydney and I was fascinated by the author's ideas and interpretations, particularly of the books of Revelation, Ezekiel and Zechariah, as well as the eschatology in Matthew's Gospel. By the time I met Graham, a few days later in Melbourne, my mind was humming with ideas, theories and questions, and I could hardly wait to tell him about what I had been reading and to have him clarify the cryptic remarks he had made on the telephone.

'What would you say,' Graham began, when the two of us were finally sitting alone over a drink, 'if you found that the world was actually being run by people who were no part whatsoever of the official governments?'

I assumed that this question was rhetorical and waited for him to continue. What he said aroused my interest still further. It appeared that Graham, too, was involved in the search for a personal truth, and his browsings had led him into a so-called Christian bookshop where he had discovered some, as he put it, 'pretty amazing stuff'. He showed me some of the books he had bought: two by Nesta Webster, published in the 1920's and called *World Revolution* and *Secret Societies and Subversive Movements*, one by Dan Smoot, published in 1962, entitled *The Invisible Government*, a large volume called *Occult Theocrasy* by Lady Queenborough, first published in 1933, and a small paperback, dated 1971, written by Gary Allen, with the title *None Dare Call It Conspiracy*.

I glanced through them and found my attention immediately focusing on the Nesta Webster books which seemed to contain a lot about Freemasonry. I agreed to read them but I asked Graham first to tell me what it was about the books that had caused him so much concern. I might have been less receptive to his reply had I not just read the Hal Lindsey books; as it was, I listened with close attention. It seemed that these writers, albeit separated in time by almost half a century, were all convinced that behind the governments of the world there operate many kinds of organisations, unknown to the public at large. These organisations wield the real power in the world and their chief interest is in world domination through financial, educational and pseudo-political means.

I was absolutely riveted by what my brother was telling

me. What he said struck some kind of chord within me and I knew I had to do some research for myself.

During that week in Melbourne I read the books Graham gave me and paid a visit to the bookshop. I found Nesta Webster's 'Secret Societies' both illuminating and disturbing. She traced the development of Freemasonry in Europe from its beginnings in the eighteenth century to the (then) present, and I learned much that I had never come across before. Furthermore, much of this was corroborated in Lady Queenborough's *Occult Theocrasy*. Despite what I felt to be an anti-semitic slant, something which I noticed in many of the works on the shelves of this 'Christian' shop, I was impressed by Miss Webster's research and intrigued by her theories on the contribution made to world revolution by secret societies, including the Freemasons. On one important point I found myself in complete harmony with the author; she drew a strong distinction between British and Continental Masonry. One of the earliest strictures laid upon me as a Freemason was that Grand Orient Freemasonry was in no way whatsoever compatible with the United Grand Lodge of England. Without being given any details, we were warned against any suggestion of amity with European Masonry, other than the Loge Nationale of France or the Scandinavian orders, and on reading this book I now began to understand why.

My brother was appalled by the whole concept of Freemasonry. Most of his knowledge of the movement had in fact come from these books and he was violent in his condemnation of it. I pointed out to him the distinction between British and Continental Masonry.

'Look, Graham,' I argued, 'even in the twenties this woman was aware of the total disparity, and it's even more defined today. We are all warned very strictly against any involvement with Grand Orient Masonry and what is more...'

I broke off, suddenly realising what I was saying. Graham was staring at me.

'What do you mean—we?' he demanded. 'You're not going to tell me you're involved in all this?'

I was certainly not going to deny something of which I was very proud, and I told my brother that I had joined the Craft some years before and that I totally refuted any accusations of heresy, political machinations or financial manipulations which anyone might choose to levy against it. Graham remained unconvinced even when I shared with him the development of my Christian philosophy and assured him that I could not now belong to any society which proscribed the Christian ethic. I would have given a lot to be able to tell him about my Lodge, about the generosity shown towards charitable causes, the decency and integrity of its members, and the constant insistence on a moral code. I very much wanted to disabuse him of the ideas he had gained from his reading, but I was uncomfortably conscious of the vows of secrecy which I'd taken, so I had to content myself with reaffirming the biblical basis of all the Masonic teaching, and to mention the existence of Christian orders within the Craft.

'In fact,' I said, 'I'm about to join one. As soon as I get back home I'm going to become a member of the Rose Croix which is....'

I got no further; my brother almost exploded with horror.

'But that's the worst of the lot!' His voice had risen and he looked extremely agitated. 'The Rose Croix ritual involves marriage with the Devil!'

I couldn't help myself; I laughed. Whatever else I had expected him to say in response to my announcement, it certainly wasn't that, and the suggestion was so preposterous that I let out a snort of mirth.

Graham, however, did not share my amusement, and I could see that he was in deadly earnest, so I did my best to calm him down and to take the heat out of the situation. I assured him that before entering the Rose Croix, I had had to sign an affidavit confirming my belief in the Holy Trinity. Graham looked at me and there was an odd expression in his eyes that I hadn't seen before.

'You wait, Ian,' he said. 'Just wait. You'll see.'

7

A Degree of Christianity?

I flew back to Britain with my mind full of what Graham and I had talked about and determined to make a closer study of the books I'd been given as well as doing some research of my own. However, the news which greeted me on my return to the office put everything else temporarily out of my mind. Tom Harvey's earlier warning to me had proved well-founded; the continental parent company of my financial backers had 'for commercial reasons' decided to withdraw most of the company's London and international placement of business and absorb it into their own account. For my company this meant an immediate loss of some 80% of the reinsurance business.

This unwelcome news was broken to me by my backers themselves. They had come to see me personally so that they could specifically reassure me of their continuing financial support. They expressed their confidence in my long-term strategy, which I had explained to them when Tom first told me of his misgivings, and although the predicted problems had come much sooner than anyone expected, I was not unduly worried by the change and was able in my turn to reassure them.

I immediately devoted all my efforts to building up the

direct insurance side of the business and set up an agency for the sole purpose of handling this, with a view to placing it with Lloyd's syndicates. I intended to use this as a way back into my own field of reinsurance, the idea being that, by putting a lot of business into Lloyd's from the direct side, I could then quite ethically ask for a share of reinsurance business from various syndicates. This, I confidently assured Henry Cavendish and Peter Lucas, my backers, would then provide them with a vehicle for future operations if the continental company were ever to take the step of severing connections totally.

I was pleased with my plan; it would benefit my own company, get me back into the area of work which I enjoyed most and repay Henry and Peter, should it become necessary, for their financial support and the confidence they had shown in me. I had it all neatly worked out; I gave Maurice, my manager, a free hand to develop the direct business to its fullest capacity, reasoning that he knew far more about it technically than I did; I introduced him to every one of our clients and potential clients and encouraged him to form close working relationships with them so that he would be totally au fait with every detail of the company's workings. Maurice was competent, highly ambitious, and I had no qualms about the company's future while he was running the development side. Everything was soon going along very smoothly and I was able to tell Henry and Peter that my strategy was working and that things would turn out very well for all of us, whatever their parent company might do in the future.

Within a comparatively short time of their announcement to me, I found that I could sit back and feel very satisfied with the status quo. I had done what I believed every good manager should do; I had planned, organised and delegated, so now I could take more of a back seat and merely keep a supervisory eye on things. Consequently the year 1982 found me with more leisure time

than I had enjoyed for some years, and I looked forward
to being able to pursue some of my own interests again,
particularly the one which by now had become the consuming passion of my life—Freemasonry.

I had progressed through the 'ranks' within my Mother
Lodge until by 1981 I had reached that of Junior Warden.
With each successive 'promotion' I had a greater part to
play at meetings and, in consequence, more words to
learn. At first I found this a dreadful problem. Never
having been very keen on any form of amateur dramatics
at school, I did not take very readily to learning lines, but
as I became more involved, so my interest grew. I became
engrossed with the ritual and memorising my words
became much easier.

I was particularly glad of this when my turn came, in my
role as Junior Warden, to deliver a fairly lengthy address
to those former Entered Apprentices who were being
raised to the Second Degree. I had to give what is called
the Lecture of the Second Tracing Board. At each Lodge
meeting three boards are displayed, one for each of the
three degrees of the Craft. Before the Lodge is opened,
that is before the meeting actually begins, the boards are
positioned so that only their blank sides are on view.
When the Lodge is opened in each degree, the board
appropriate to that degree is turned to display the design.
As part of the addresses after the candidate's initiation or
raising, the intricate designs on the appropriate board are
explained to him.

When you are the candidate yourself you tend to take
in very little of what is being explained to you. I found that
it was only when I had to do the explaining myself that I
really absorbed it all, and very fascinating I found it. All
the lectures are aimed at explaining the bases on which
Freemasonry is formed and operates. The Second Degree
Tracing Board, on which I had to speak, depicts the two
great pillars at the entrance to Solomon's temple, with a

large winding staircase and various other designs and symbols. The lecture includes an explanation of how the word 'Shibboleth' came to be used as a password by the early masons during the building of the temple and comprises something in the region of a thousand words. I was determined to be word-perfect in my delivery. I had sat through some ceremonies which were, to my mind, totally spoilt by the participants' lack of preparation, and I resolved that when my turn came to speak, I would do myself and Lutine Lodge proud. To that end I carried a copy of the lecture around with me, and whenever I had a spare moment I studied it. On the night, I did manage to achieve my goal and got through the whole thing without faltering. Unfortunately, in my anxiety to do it well, I also went through it with scarcely a pause for breath, so that the result was a lecture delivered at breakneck speed to a somewhat bemused candidate. However this minor detail did not prevent senior members of the Lodge from congratulating me on my diligence and I felt glad that I had taken such trouble to memorise my part in the evening's proceedings.

I did not realise it at the time but that diligence was to count very much to my credit in the Lodge. It had revealed my interest in ritual and my seriousness about the Craft, and was to lead to my being approached later with invitations to join other orders. In the meantime I was looking forward to completing the third degree of Craft Masonry by joining the Royal Arch.

The Holy Royal Arch has a history which goes back to the early days of Masonry and is generally regarded as the ultimate in the Craft. My exaltation into Chapter, to use the formal terminology, took place towards the end of my seventh year as a Freemason and was, in terms of drama at least, one of the most impressive ceremonies I underwent. I was, as on previous occasions, blindfolded and led through a series of questions and answers, culminating in the familiar 'having been kept for a considerable time in a state of darkness, what, in your present condition, is the predominant wish of your heart?' to which I made the prescribed response—'light'.

This was now the fourth occasion on which I had taken part as a candidate in a ritual, and I had also been present at many other initiations, so I was taking the whole thing quite calmly, but I was totally unprepared for the spectacle which greeted my eyes when the blindfold came off. I seemed to be in an underground cavern, looking down a long tunnel at the end of which stood a tall figure in flowing robes. He was holding a long staff and in the dim light of the place I was conscious of a red glow all about him. For a split second I had the impression that I had been transported to some great vaulted chamber into the presence of an august being. As my eyes adjusted, I took in my surroundings and realised what I was actually seeing: twelve men, in two lines of six, were standing facing each other; each carried a long pole from which hung a triangular pennant, or guidon bearing emblems of the twelve tribes of Israel, and these were tilted towards each other to form an arch. The only light came from strategically placed candles; one glowing at the far end illuminated the red robes of the Principal who, I could now see, was flanked by two other officers, each holding a similar sceptre with which they framed him. The whole effect was quite breathtaking and very skilfully achieved. I realised that Masonic ritual still held a lot of surprises, and the Royal Arch ceremony had whetted my appetite for more.

It was during this ceremony of exaltation into the Royal Arch that I first heard the reference to 'the sacred and mysterious name of the true and living God'. This name, according to Masonic doctrine, was among the deep and significant secrets that had been lost with the untimely death of 'our Master, Hiram Abiff'. This important personage was, supposedly, the 'skilful craftsman' mentioned in the Old Testament, who was sent by Hiram, King of Tyre, to mastermind the building of King Solomon's temple, and it is on this legend that the theme of the Craft is based. Each degree has its own ritual enacting part of the story and during the Royal Arch ritual the sacred name is revealed as 'Jah-Bul-On'[1] and that name, together with the name 'Jehovah', is recited in a series of syllables by the candidate and two officers of the Chapter towards the close of his initiation. I found this mixing up of the two words rather confusing but got through it with the assistance of my companions. The ceremony and play-acting which happens at meetings is used to instruct modern-day Masons in morality, to show them a pattern for a life of integrity. As my attitude to the Christian church altered, and I began drawing parallels between Masonic codes of conduct and the teachings of Jesus, I began to inquire amongst my fellow Masons about the Christian orders which I had heard existed, and these inquiries eventually led to an invitation to join one of them, the Rose Croix.

The prospect of joining a Christian order was very appealing, and I was looking forward to learning new, and I expected, different ritual. Before the date fixed for my 'exaltation' I had had to sign a declaration, affirming my faith in the Holy Trinity and as I had now come to the point where I considered myself a Christian, I did this gladly.

The most significant difference between the ritual of the Rose Croix and that of the Craft degrees is the Christian, as opposed to Old Testament, symbolism. The candidate is told that Masonry is in a state of despair because of the loss of the Word, and that his help is needed in its recovery. The ensuing ceremony takes the form of a journey to find this Word, and this was all explained to me by the Sovereign, the quivalent of a Worshipful Master, in the darkened room where my search began. Unlike in the

Craft initiations, I was not blindfolded and was aware of others around me, but between me and the Sovereign was a veil making it impossible for me to see him. I was told that I had thirty-three days to find the Word (thirty-three being the age of Jesus at his death) and that my first destination was the three pillars of Wisdom, Strength and Beauty. Here, at least, I was on familiar ground; in the Craft lectures we are told that Masonic buildings are supported by these pillars, which represent God's wisdom, his omnipotence, and the beauty of his creation.

The Sovereign went on to tell me of the help I could get in my search from the New Covenant, the one brought in by Jesus supposedly to replace the one made by God with Abraham, and I set off on my circuits of the room. As I walked, one of the officers began reading from the Bible; it was that part of the book of Isaiah which foretells the suffering and death of Christ. During my 'journey' I was given three metal plaques, each bearing one of the letters F, H and C, and on my return to the Sovereign, my escort, who was known as the Marshal, reported that I had not been able to find the Word but that I had discovered that the three pillars had been changed into the Christian virtues of Faith, Hope and Charity.

The Sovereign congratulated me on my discovery and told me that I must now take the Obligation. At this point, the veil which had been across the room was drawn back to reveal an altar on which there was a representation of Calvary, that is a grouping of three crosses. The tallest one, in the centre, was decorated with a rose and a crown of thorns and the altar frontal bore embroidered pictures of five swords.

I took the Obligation, swearing both secrecy and allegiance to the Supreme Council, with my hand on a New Testament which I saw was open at the beginning of John's Gospel, and I began to understand that the lost word for which I was searching was in fact the 'Logos' of

John. As I made the vows, a sword and a pair of compasses were placed across my hand, to remind me, it was explained, of the three essentials of my life—my Christian beliefs, my personal honour and my Masonry.

My Obligation completed, I was led across the room and for the first time could see, in the candlelight, the diagram on the floor around which I had walked. In the centre was a pelican, plucking blood from its breast, and around this were seven white rings. The Sovereign explained that six of these represent the six days of creation, and the seventh foretells eternity when the Messiah will return to earth and all men will be judged. He continued with an explanation of the Christian virtues during which I recognised many quotations from the well known passage in the First Epistle to the Corinthians, which begins, in the King James or Authorized Version, 'Though I speak with the tongues of men and of angels, and have not charity....'

At the close of this oration there was a general exodus through one of the doors in the room, but as I made to follow, I was gently restrained and reminded that I had not yet found the Word. A veil was placed over my head and shoulders, the veil of mourning, and I was taken through another door and left 'to contemplate'. The first thing I saw through the veil was a skull on the floor at my feet. I gazed at the macabre object for some moments and tried to repress a shudder. I guessed that the subject of my contemplation was supposed to be my own mortality, and that the skull was a grim reminder of it.

Eventually, rather to my relief, the door opened and I was greeted by 'Raphael', the angel who was to guide me for the rest of my journey. He told me that I had been travelling through the valley of the shadow of death but, because I had found the three Christian virtues, I could now continue with my journey and he would lead me into the Mansions of Light.

I was not sorry to be leaving the darkened room; it had had a chilling atmosphere which I found extremely uncomfortable, and had reminded me of the uncertainty I had felt at moments in my very first initiation ceremony. Together with my guide I passed through the door and suddenly I was surrounded by a blaze of colour; everything around me seemed to be red, a strong crimson red, which was quite stunningly bright after the darkness of the 'valley'. On the red carpet in front of me was a ladder strewn with red roses, and Raphael led me to its foot. He reported on my 'journey' to the Sovereign, and I was instructed to ascend the ladder. As I did so, each of the steps was explained to me. On the first three steps I 'found' Faith, Hope and Charity, and on the last four I discovered, at last, parts of the Word, the subject of my quest.

What I was actually given were four more letters, printed on card, and as I picked up each one, verses from the Bible were read aloud, describing Christ's life on earth. I gave the letters to the Sovereign and he congratulated me on my success. Mourning was no longer necessary so the veil was removed so that I might see my discovery in all its splendour. I had by now realised what the four letters spelt, and as the Sovereign arranged them in their correct order, I was conscious of a vague sense of disappointment. The letters spelt 'INRI', the inscription over Jesus' cross, and although I had identified Jesus as the 'Word' I was seeking, I nevertheless was expecting something of which I had hitherto been completely ignorant, rather like the name 'Jah-Bul-On' which I had learned in the Royal Arch. I had come across the word 'INRI' which stood for the Latin equivalent of 'Jesus of Nazareth, King of the Jews', many times in churches and in books; why was it so secret? I immediately assumed that there must be some deeper significance to it than I had known and waited expectantly for the next part of the proceedings.

The Prelate of the Chapter, who had been reading the Bible extracts during the ceremony, now moved with the letters to the altar and placed them on a Cubic stone which was positioned so as to link three triangles of lights. Everyone knelt and paid homage to the Word, which was now surrounded by these emblems of the Trinity. I was summoned to kneel in front of the altar, and received my accolade as a Knight of the Pelican and Eagle. This was followed by a touch on my forehead with a seal which was engraved with a rose, and I was thus ennobled as a 'Prince of the Order of the Rose Croix of Heredom'.

As the Sovereign took my hands and raised me to my feet, I felt a sense of elation, of exultation almost, that I had taken another step forward in Masonry, and a significant one at that. Of the thirty-three degrees in Masonry, I had now, by this evenings proceedings, reached the eighteenth. Furthermore, in my Craft Lodge I was only a year or so away from becoming the Worshipful Master, and in my mind that was the real gateway to the innermost secrets of the movement, which would reveal to me such deep scriptural and spiritual truths as most professed Christians had never imagined.

I listened with rapt attention to the explanations of the symbolism of the Collar and Jewel with which I was now invested, and on the other features of the degree which were quite new to me. The pelican, which I had seen earlier, traditionally tore its breast to revive its young with its own blood, and in the Rose Croix symbolises the Saviour who shed his blood to save man from death. The eagle represents the strength and domination of God; the rose, which has many symbolic attributes including love and beauty, becomes in Masonry, the Rose of Sharon and the Lily of the Valley, flowers which are not precisely identifiable but which are named in the Song of Solomon.

For the Rose Croix Mason, I was informed, it is the sign of the Perfection and Passion of Our Lord.

Following the explanations of all the signs, tokens and words, I was led by the Marshal to the West side of the room and my new Masonic titles were proclaimed. I felt proud, exhilarated and, deep inside, a sense of profound satisfaction.

'This is what real Christianity is all about,' I told myself as we were ushered from the room while it was prepared for the final part of the evening's proceedings.

The Sovereign and Prelate remained, together with two other members of the Chapter, whom I knew to be thirty-third degree Masons and members of the Supreme Council, the nine-member governing body of the British Jurisdiction of the Rose Croix. What secrets and truths these men had discovered in their Masonic progress I could only speculate, but I knew that whatever these might be, I wanted desperately to find them myself.

We returned to the red room and formed a circle. The Sovereign was standing before the altar on which I could see a chalice and plate and I prepared to take Communion with a sense of pleasure at this, as I saw, fitting conclusion to a Christian evening.

The plate began its journey round the circle, starting with the Sovereign and ending at me, the latest member. I watched, in order not to break any prescribed pattern. I saw that each man in turn took a biscuit from the plate, broke it and shared it with his immediate neighbour who had turned to face him; they then dipped the biscuit into something in the centre of the plate, and ate. When it finally arrived at me, I took the proffered piece, dipped it and raised it to my mouth. The taste of the salt made me recoil involuntarily. I had not expected that. What role did salt have in a Christian communion? As far as I knew, the rituals where salt played a part were all... I suddenly heard Graham's voice, warning me about mysterious organisations. I swallowed hard, feeling the unpleasant dryness in my throat. The cup was on its way to me. It was large and double-handled like a sporting trophy. I waited, listening to the words exchanged. The cup was with my neighbour; he drank and held it towards me.

'Emmanuel,' he said.

'Pax vobiscum,' I responded and bowed my head to the cup. As I saw the white wine, something inside me, deep and unnamable, rebelled and cried out silently, 'This is wrong!' I raised my head from the cup and glanced about me. All I could see in that moment were eyes watching me. Thoughts raced through my mind: these men here were all friends, I knew them to be good, Christian-living people; they could not conceivably be involved in anything intrinsically wrong; I was getting myself worked up over nothing. This ritual with the salt and the white wine might not have been what I was expecting, but this, after all, was a Masonic gathering, not a church service, and therefore the emblems must have a special meaning and significance of their own, which would later be made clear to me. I lowered my head and drank. I was the last of the circle to do so and I passed the chalice back to the Sovereign who pronounced the words 'All is consumed'. Everyone around me made a response in Latin, and the Sovereign moved towards the altar. Taking up the four letters which had earlier been placed there 'that it [the Word] might not be exposed to the eyes of the profane but be consumed according to ancient custom', he placed them in another chalice which the Prelate held out to him. The Prelate then took a lighted taper and set fire to the Word. As it burned with a fiery red flame he pronounced 'Consummatum est'—('It is finished'), Christ's words from the cross.

As the Prelate delivered the closing oration all my earlier reservations seemed suddenly ludicrous to me. I heard that the Resurrection had taken place, that the

Saviour had appeared in all his glory, that all burdens were now lifted from our hearts and that we had received a new commandment, that is to love one another. The closing word of the ceremony was 'Emmanuel'—'God with us'. I was filled with a sense of reassurance; all was well; God was with us.

'What a pity,' I thought as I mingled with my smiling brothers, receiving their warm congratulations, that Sally could not experience all this. Sally, with her conventional churchgoing would never, by virtue of her sex, be privy to the kind of secrets waiting to be revealed to me and to those other enlightened men who were prepared to seek for the real truth in the complex degrees of Freemasonry.

Note

[1] See note page 179.

8

Reflections

The closing minutes of the Rose Croix ritual had suddenly brought everything that my brother Graham had said right into the forefront of my mind. Our long discussions out in Melbourne had disturbed me more than a little, and, although I had discounted his views on Freemasonry, I could not help but give some credence to the claims of Nesta Webster, Dan Smoot and especially Gary Allen regarding subversive movements aimed at world domination, in view of what I had already found in the Hal Lindsey books.

I had by this time concluded that Jesus Christ was God incarnate, but it was very much an intellectual conclusion and I had not yet grasped the concept of any sort of divine plan for the world in which Jesus figured. When I read *Satan is Alive and Well on Planet Earth* many things suddenly began to make sense to me; for instance, why, accepting the existence of a Creator who embodied love, there was such evil rampant in the world. The lengthy conversations I'd had with my mother over the years had acquainted me with occultism in its many and varied forms, and I now began to get my first impressions of a struggle for world supremacy between the forces of good and evil. When Graham, just at the same time, produced the writings he had found on the subject of secret, behind-the-scenes governments and suchlike, it was as though parts of a jigsaw were slowly sliding into place. In particular, the Book of Revelation which I had hitherto regarded as little more than mystical mumbo-jumbo, suddenly took on a new significance for me; I began to appreciate its place in the scriptures and to feel that we, mankind, were merely pawns in some great game of cosmic chess. It made my forthcoming entry into a Christian order of Freemasonry more attractive than ever; I felt as though I was not only giving myself some sort of protection in the face of an ever-spreading evil, but also that, on entry into these orders, more and more scriptural secrets of the type expounded in Lindsey's books, would be disclosed to me.

The incident during my 'perfection' as a Prince of the Order of the Rose Croix when I, expecting to take the bread and red wine of Holy Communion, was confronted instead by biscuits, salt and white wine, had recalled all my brother's misgivings, and everything he had said was very much in my mind as I set about re-reading the books he had given me, and undertaking some research of my own. Although I was intrigued by the whole of this new dimension which I was exploring, the question that concerned me most was how Freemasonry figured in all of it. My brother was convinced that Freemasonry was, of itself, intrinsically evil, but knowing what I did I could not accept that the movement in Britain was anything other than a soundly-based organisation of men of the highest integrity, which constituted a considerable force for good, or at least good works, in this country.

The European movement was however quite another matter, and I had been made aware from my earliest days in the Craft that there was no amity between the United Grand Lodge of England and Grand Orient Masonry. Through my research I learned about the origins of this movement and of the existence of other organisations and individuals previously unknown to me, such as Adam Weishaupt, the founder of a secret society called the Bavarian Illuminati, and General Albert Pike, who was a practising Luciferian whilst at the same time Sovereign Grand Commander of the Southern Jurisdiction, USA, of the Rose Croix, in the latter half of the last century. I also reacquainted myself with a certain Madame Blavatsky, the founder of the Theosophical Society, about whom I had heard at length from my mother. I summarise my researches and the conclusions I came to in a later chapter; what interested me most at this time, almost to the point of obsession, was the world situation looked at from a prophetic standpoint and I became convinced that the 'end times' referred to in the Bible, were now relatively near at hand, particularly in view of the fact that, with the creation of the state of Israel in 1948, the Jews were now 'back in the land'.

In the midst of all this fermenting mass of confusion and strife, I saw Freemasonry as a bastion against the oncoming tide of evil and I was sure that as I progressed further through the higher degrees, I would receive more and more enlightenment. Whatever the darker side of some continental Masonry might be, I drew a clear distinction between it and what I was involved in. I remembered my mother telling me not to lump everyone who practised witchcraft together in one category, because (she claimed) there were white witches who worked for good, as well as the black variety who practised evil. That was how I now regarded Freemasonry, with British Masonry very much as the white witch in a dark world.

I was not very pleased, therefore, to be told by my younger brother John that some of the emblems used on Masonic regalia were actually occultic. He was staying with me for a few days and had picked up a book which I had acquired from the Masonic publishers, giving details of Masonic Orders which come after the degree of Master Mason.

'Look at this,' he said, pointing to an illustration of the jewels belonging to the Order of Allied Masonic Degrees. 'Pure occult!'

'What utter rubbish!' I said, with some indignation. 'You're as bad as Graham. Everything's occultic in his opinion.'

'I don't know why the word offends you,' said John. 'Occult only means hidden, after all, and everything about Freemasonry is hidden or secret, isn't it?'

I was not mollified; to me occult meant only one thing—evil. I did not take kindly to the suggestion that there was any connection between it and Freemasonry. Both my brothers were totally misguided, I believed. John was now a member of the Theosophical Society and in an attempt to convince me of the harmlessness of the word which I so abhorred, he took me to the Society's bookshop where I found an incredibly varied range of subjects from the Egyptian Book of the Dead to a fascinating work called *The Secret Teachings of All Ages*, which caught my interest immediately.

Somewhat to my surprise I also found on the shelves a volume called *Darkness Visible* which reproduces the actual words used in Masonic ceremonies. As all the ceremonies in which I had been involved were shrouded in secrecy which we were strictly abjured not to break, I was amazed to find such an exact reproduction of the ritual freely available for anyone to read. On reading it through with great care I was glad that I found nothing in it to cause me to alter my opinions as to the fundamental purpose and the essential integrity of the organisation. As far as I was concerned, by becoming a Freemason I had embarked upon a path which would lead me to the truth for which so many people search in vain. I was sorry for both my brothers in their ignorance and determined to go as far as I possibly could in the movement in my quest for enlightenment.

9

The Crashing Blow

In March 1983, nine years after my initiation into the Craft, I was installed as Worshipful Master of Lutine Lodge. It was something I had looked forward to since my first entry into the Craft and I cannot describe the pleasure I felt on that evening as I was led to the Master's chair and took my place surrounded by friends and well-wishers. I remembered my first entry into the Captain's Room, following my initiation ceremony; all the same faces were there, and many new ones, and the atmosphere was as cordial and relaxed as it had been then. Truly, the Masonic movement was a marvellous institution, and I thanked Providence for the day I had first mentioned my interest in it to Hamish Morrison.

I was looking forward to a busy and enjoyable year of Masonic activity, for as well as being Master of my Mother Lodge, I held the positions of Assistant Sojourner in the Royal Arch, Raphael in the Rose Croix, and Captain of Guards in the Knights Templar. I had also become acquainted with Mark Masonry, which is one of the oldest grades of Freemasonry, and grew out of an ancient ceremony in which each craftsman selected his own personal mark to designate his work. My guides and mentors on the Craft had assured me that Mark Masonry would form an essential balance in my Masonic career and in January I was admitted to a Mark Lodge. The following May I joined its appendant Order, the Royal Ark Mariners whose ritual related to the story of the Flood. My interest in the Christian Orders grew, and in the same month that I became Master of the Lodge, I was installed as a Knight of the Red Cross of Constantine. In November I was admitted to the Order of the Knights of the Holy Sepulchre, and during the same year I joined, by invitation, two other Craft lodges, one being my old school lodge, Charterhouse, and the other, one of the Stewards', or Red Apron, lodges.

I was a completely dedicated and totally committed Freemason and I loved it! I loved the whole thing—the camaraderie, the exclusivity, the wining and dining after each meeting, but most of all I loved the ritual. The more I had to learn, the better I liked it. I loved the rather quaint formality of the language used in the Craft ceremonies, and even more the solemn beauty of the Christian rituals. My favourite degree was the Rose Croix; it was so very diverse and interesting, as well as being, I felt, based immovably on Jesus Christ.

By this time I had intellectually made the link between the Old and New Testaments and had concluded that Jesus was, in truth, God incarnate. The full implications of this, however, were still lost on me, and following our move from All Saints Church, my attitude to orthodox religion was again fast hardening. The more alive and meaningful Masonic ritual appeared, the more hollow and fossilised seemed the rites of the Anglican Church. Each Sunday I accompanied Sally and the children, now four in number since the arrival of Kirstie, to St Dunstan's church, and each time I emerged with a growing sense of dissatisfaction. It was in Freemasonry that I found my only real satisfaction and delight.

The business, meanwhile, scarcely seemed to need my

attention at all. The atmosphere in the office was relaxed and happy, and everyone seemed to work very well together. I had added to my staff a retired Lloyd's underwriter who worked alongside Maurice Collighan in attracting business into the company for us to channel into Lloyd's. I liked Maurice's attitude; he was supremely confident about the future, and I saw no reason to doubt his judgement, so I went ahead with investing in the expensive equipment necessary to cope with the amount of business we expected. The fact that this business was not coming in as quickly as we would have liked did not cause me any undue concern and I assured Henry Cavendish, at one of our regular meetings, that I had every confidence in my manager, and that I saw no reason to doubt that he himself could be absorbed into the company at any time he chose.

By this time, Henry had severed almost completely his ties with the continental company and was operating in a private capacity, looking for a *modus operandi* within the City while administering the run-off of his own underwriting agency. I anticipated that it would not be long before he joined us, and the prospect pleased me. After all, it was Henry who had been the means of my starting up on my own, and now that his circumstances had altered so drastically, it seemed quite fitting that I should repay his confidence in me by taking him into my company.

In the summer of 1983, I became aware that relations between my two longest-standing employees, Tom Harvey and Maurice himself, were not as happy as I had believed. Things came to a head between the two men in a way that could only have one outcome. This was the first ripple in what had been a serene pool, and because I trusted Maurice's judgement, I came to the decision that, to restore that former serenity, Tom would have to go. It was a decision I regretted having to make—after all, we had been together from the beginning, but I relied a great deal on Maurice and I did not want to jeopardise the future success of the company. To make matters worse, Tom's severance proved to be acrimonious and expensive at a time when we could ill afford it.

In order to channel business into Lloyd's, it had been necessary for me to form ties with a broking house under whose name I could operate. The first of these arrangements had ended with a tremendous personality clash between Maurice and the directors, and we were now linked with another long-established house and were looking forward to a future merger. Some time after Tom's departure, Maurice came to me with a proposition about the company's future which rather took me aback. He told me that a business acquaintance of his, a young man whom he had known for some years, was now acting as major domo, a sort of front man, for a large Arab consortium who wished to buy into Lloyd's. The proposition was that they would buy out both my company and the Lloyd's broking house whom we used, inject a large amount of direct international business, merge the two and leave me and my company to run operations.

Although this approach came more or less out of the blue, I was quite happy to look into the proposals, and at first they did look promising; there would be excellent salaries for myself and Maurice, a large injection of business and seemingly unending funds from the Arabs. The only snag was that in this new arrangement there would be no room for Henry, and I baulked at that. The deal would mean that he could recover most of his financial outlay from the last four years, but I nevertheless felt that I would be committing an act of betrayal, as though, faced with the prospect of a sudden influx of funds, I was ready to discount all his former support.

I tried my best to persuade the consortium to alter their plans to include Henry, but they were adamant, and as negotiations continued, I found that my reservations about the deal were increasing. The young man I was negotiating with was very much of the type I least admired in business and I was not happy at the prospect of my company being dominated by someone who shared the attitude, prevalent in the city, of worshipping at the altar of big business. Everything was subservient to the business ethic, and that approach was not the one which I employed in my office. My staff knew this, and together we had made our office life into something that was almost an extension of family life. The incident with Tom was the only unhappy note in an otherwise relaxed and convivial atmosphere, and I fervently hoped that nothing of the kind would occur again. If I were to be answerable to a man with a completely different code of conduct, how would I cope?

While these discussions were going on, Henry was making final preparations to join my company. The severance from his continental parent company now being complete, he was about to join us as Financial Adviser in our recently acquired new premises, bringing his own personal secretary with him. I did not mention the Arab consortium's proposal until after I had finally rejected it, and when I did, I found, to my horror, that Henry was aghast at my decision. He was far from happy with the financial position of the company, which he was now funding from his privately owned business, and would have been more than content to cut his losses and withdraw. I had committed the classic error of doing totally the wrong thing for all the right reasons. Henry tried to resurrect the issue with the consortium, but it was too late; the chance had gone.

It was now December and the Masonic season was in full swing, taking up much of my time and energy. At the office, Henry was having a great deal of difficulty finding his niche, and was growing more and more unhappy with the state of the finances. Pressure was growing for the company to stand on its own feet but little of the business which Maurice had so confidently predicted had materialised. An attempted merger with another Lloyd's broking house, whose chairman was a friend of Henry's, came to nothing and the New Year found us still afloat but with time running out. I was still not unduly worried about the long term. All businesses, I reasoned, have their rough patches, and my confidence in Maurice remained unshaken. While sharing his concern over the delay, I felt certain that all our plans would soon come to fruition in an influx of direct business which would lift us all out of the doldrums and set us well and truly on our planned route.

I repeated these optimistic views to Henry when, in January, he took Maurice and me to lunch with a business-consultant friend of his, but both men remained unimpressed, and it soon became clear from the conversation that I was by now regarded as a millstone round the company's neck. It was put to me that I might take a nine-month sabbatical in order to relieve the strain on the resources to a certain degree.

I was aghast at the suggestion. There was no way I could afford to take unpaid leave of that length. Since starting the company I had taken only enough salary to meet my living needs, so I had no large amount of capital in the bank, or anywhere else, on which I could draw. Furthermore, I saw no real reason why I should leave, even temporarily, at this juncture. Although, as Chief Executive, I took ultimate responsibility, I knew that the slow materialisation of business was not directly attributable to any fault on my part, and that my overall strategy had been sound. I was being asked to abandon something which I had founded, nurtured and developed, something which was part of myself. A sabbatical was out of the question.

So, I declared, was allowing Henry to buy me out, a proposal which he put forward after my rejection of the sabbatical idea. I knew I had the support of Maurice in my desire to stay on and bring the business through this sticky patch. He had given me every indication that if I were to go, he would also resign and, as he put it, take most of the business with him. All in all, I saw no reason why I should be pressured into giving up my child, which is how I regarded my company, and I said as much to Henry.

In February, Henry left for a holiday in Portugal, during which he hoped to think the situation through and make some clear decisions. On his return he called a Board meeting. With perfect timing, I had succumbed to a flu virus that was going around, and I had to drag myself into London, with a thumping head, sore throat and streaming eyes. Promptly at ten there was a tap at my door and Henry entered, accompanied by his secretary and followed, not only by Maurice and his assistant, but by most of the staff as well. Henry took the chair and delivered a sort of 'state of the union' message, detailing the company's problems, its financial position and so forth. He finished speaking and invited me to reply. I glanced around at my colleagues; without exception they looked sombre and ill at ease. I responded to Henry's address with a defence of my own strategy, accepting that the present position was rather bleak, but confident that Maurice's efforts would soon reap their rewards and that business would come in as planned.

'And I know,' I said, firmly, 'that Maurice agrees with me in this and will support me in what I'm saying.'

I paused, and looked across at Maurice. He seemed intent on studying the pattern on the carpet and would not meet my eyes. It was then that I realised the truth—I was on my own.

Henry waited until I had sat down then proceeded in a few short sentences to make it very clear who it was that he held responsible for the situation. All the present ills of the company were laid at my door, my resignation was asked for, and the meeting brought to a close.

As quietly as they had entered, my staff left. Nobody other than Henry and I had uttered a word. His secretary who had taken the minutes, gathered up her papers and almost ran from the room, an expression of profound distress on her face. Henry rose to his feet and moved towards the door.

'I'll see you shortly, Ian,' he said, 'to tidy things up.'

A few hours later, I emerged into the freezing London street, shivering in the icy February wind. Things had indeed been tidied up; I had been declared redundant, with a month's salary in lieu of notice and allowed, by way of compensation, to keep my company car. That was all. I was finished. I got into my car and pointed it in the direction of home.

IO

Unexpected Meeting

By the time I eventually turned the car into my own drive, my throat felt as though it had been sand-papered, my eyes were aching with the effort of concentrating on the darkened road and my headache was well on the way to becoming the worst I had ever experienced. Everything had begun to seem quite unreal, and even as I heard my own voice recounting the day's events to Sally, I felt as though it had all happened to someone else. Sally could see that my reactions were severely affected by my physical condition, and she insisted that I go to bed and let the wretched flu take its course. When I emerged a couple of days later I felt much more human, but still somehow removed from reality. It was as though I was looking at things through the wrong end of a telescope. In a strange way I felt a sensation of relief; the tensions between Henry and myself that had built up over the preceding few months had affected me more than I'd realised and it was as though the valve had at last been opened on a pressure-cooker, and all the seething and bubbling had ceased.

I had lost my company; that was bad, but not the end of the world. I had been reduced to the ranks of the unemployed in a particularly unpleasant and painful way, but I could soon remedy the situation. I had plenty of contacts

in the City, and with my background and experience I saw
no problem in finding another job fairly easily. I would
take a breather, just a short break, spend some time
preparing a curriculum vitae, and putting out a few
feelers; nothing too frantic, as I was still feeling pretty
washed-out after the flu; I wouldn't rush about too much.
I went up to London, and a friend let me use his office as a
temporary base from where I could telephone around and
set up some meetings. He was very sympathetic and very
encouraging about the future. I saw no reason whatsoever
to panic.

I might have remained in this state of shock-induced
detachment indefinitely but for two things—the car and
the phone call. One of the first things Sally had said when
we sat down to discuss the situation, was that the Mercedes would have to go. She had already been contacted
by Henry, requesting an immediate return of the Volvo
Estate which she used for ferrying the children around to
their various schools, and the Mercedes, with its very high
fuel consumption and servicing costs would be pro-
hibitively expensive. It would have to be exchanged for
something more suitable. To come to a sensible decision
was one thing; to act on it quite another. I found myself
very reluctant to approach the local car dealers with my
beautiful prestige saloon and look at more modest mod-
els. It was Sally who finally took the keys and drove the
Mercedes into the nearest town. She eventually returned
to report that she had done a deal and I could accompany
her back to the garage and collect our new vehicle. I think
it was at the moment when I eased myself behind the
wheel of the small Renault that the protective bubble, in
which I seemed to have been living since the board meeting, burst, and the reality of the situation began to seep
through to me. Depression, mixed with resentment,
started its insidious work inside me, and that evening,
long after the family had all gone to bed, I sat staring into

space, reliving that horrible day when all that I had worked for had crumbled around me.

After the close of the meeting I had begun clearing my desk and sorting out my papers, working automatically without really noticing what I was doing. Henry's private secretary, who had been so distressed during the meeting, came into my office and, giving me a hug, told me how disgusted she was at what she called the cold-blooded, dispassionate act of destruction she had just witnessed.

'I can't carry on working here after that,' she said. 'I'm looking for another job. I'm so sorry, Ian.'

One by one during the rest of the day, the other members of my staff came in and expressed their regrets at what had happened.

When I finally went in to see Henry, I found him as calm and businesslike as ever. Everything had been neatly arranged for my departure; just how neatly I only fully realised later. I took legal advice about my position, but was told to 'take the car and go quietly', as I would fare no better if I appealed to any sort of tribunal. Henry had covered himself and the company against any possible financial claim I might make, and now, here I was, ten days later, having 'gone quietly', without the car, and with my bank balance dwindling fast.

I went over and over all this in my mind for the whole of the evening and when I finally went to bed, more and more recollections of that day came crowding into my mind. Sleep was impossible. Any sense of detachment had gone; I was back in the real world with a vengeance. Here I was, with a large house to run, a hefty mortgage round my neck, a family of six people to feed and clothe, four lots of school fees to pay and—no money, no job. How could it have happened?

I lay there in the dark, brooding on the unfairness of it all, and got up next morning, heavy eyed and short-tempered. It was Thursday 8th March, 1984. At eleven o'clock the phone rang. It was Keith, Maurice's assistant. The call lasted some ten minutes and when I put the receiver down I found Sally watching me rather warily.

'What did he want?' she asked.

'Keith,' I answered, speaking slowly and distinctly, 'felt that he ought to put me in the picture about what's been happening. He wanted to fill me in on the background to that little performance last week. You see, it appears they all knew; all the staff; they knew what was going to happen at the meeting. Henry had told them all to be there in my office without fail.'

Sally looked at me, incredulously.

'You mean they were all aware of what Henry was going to do? And no one warned you?'

'Apparently they were under instructions not to. Henry spoke to them all after he came back from Portugal and explained that the survival of the company, that is the continuance of their jobs, depended upon my going.'

I could hear Keith's voice, defensive, apologetic: 'I didn't like it, Ian. No one did. But I was worried; I've got a family and a mortgage and...' His voice tailed off. 'If I'd known that he was going to do it the way he did, I might have said something. Anyway, for what it's worth, I feel rotten about the whole business, and I thought you ought to know.'

'Keith thought I ought to know,' I repeated woodenly to Sally. I recalled the meeting, the strange, sombre silence. It made sense now.

'They had all been told that their jobs were on the line if they said anything at all to back me up.'

'Even Maurice?' asked Sally.

'Especially Maurice.' But even as I spoke the words I could not believe them. The others, perhaps, but not Maurice; surely he had had enough confidence in himself and in me to make a stand. He had given me enough assurances about the company's future; what had changed? What had Henry said to silence him? What had Henry worked out in his cool, calculating brain to achieve his own ends?

All that day I sat staring at the wall. Inside me was a feeling I did not recognise. As I went over and over the events of the last months, that feeling began to grow. I remembered Henry's stony silence when I told him I had turned down the Arabs' proposals because they did not include him; I heard him suggesting I take a long sabbatical, offering to buy me out, complaining that there was no real niche for him within my organisation. Why had I not seen it? He must have planned it all, I told myself, because he wanted the company for himself. As this idea flashed into my troubled mind I grasped at it and hung on; the feeling that had begun inside me welled up and I recognised it for what it was—it was hatred, a deep, intense, burning hatred, and its object was Henry Cavendish.

He was the reason, I told myself, why I had lost everything; the reason why I had been subjected to that humiliating castigation in front of my staff, the reason why my whole world now lay in ruins. By the time midnight came, I could hardly see anything except Henry's face in front of me. I was sick with hate. I lay in bed, staring at the ceiling but seeing only Henry. Sally had finally fallen asleep, exhausted, but I was wider awake than I had ever been in my life.

Suddenly, like an icy knife cutting through the hot, red mist of anger and loathing, a cold, clear thought came into my head. I knew what I had to do to calm this ghastly turmoil inside me, an anaesthetic for the burning pain I was feeling. I would have to take my revenge on the man who had caused it. I would kill Henry. Even as the idea came I rejected it. Killing him was not the answer; if he were dead he wouldn't be able to feel anything and I wanted him very much to be able to feel something, to share this hurt of mine, this incredible feeling of loss that had overtaken me in the last twenty-four hours. I felt like a mother who had had her child forcibly taken away from her, a child she had borne and nurtured and was proud of. I would make Henry share this pain with me.

Lying there in the dark I formed my plan: I would destroy something Henry loved, then he too would know what it was like. I would kill his wife. It would be quite easy; I knew where they lived; I knew the house; I would break in and take Henry by surprise while he was asleep. It would then be an easy matter to overpower him and render him helpless. That done, I would proceed to murder his wife in front of his eyes. I would do this in the most humiliating and degrading way I could devise and after it was over I would turn my attentions to him. I would not kill him, I would not risk damaging his mental faculties, because then he might not be able to recall what he had had to live through; he might forget what he had seen and heard this night. Instead, I would leave him maimed and helpless, a useless, speechless cripple for the rest of his life, but his brain, that brilliant financial brain, that cool, calculating brain which had so cleverly engineered my destruction, would continue to function as before, unable to blot out the memory of the horror, the blood, the pain.

I was intoxicated with my plan. This was what I needed to bring peace into my raging mind, to deaden this unbearable pain. I looked at the clock, the figures glowing in the dark; it was 2 am. I would get up, collect the axe which we kept for splitting logs and go now. Cautiously, so as not to disturb Sally, I began to sit up, but as I did so, I became aware of something touching me, restraining me. A hand was pressing on my chest, gently but firmly preventing me from rising. I was about to begin struggling with this unseen hindrance when out of the blackness a voice spoke.

'Ian! Stop it!'

I turned my head to where the voice came from. In the darkness of the room I could make out the shape of a man, standing next to my bed.

'Who the bloody hell are you?' I demanded in a fury, and he spoke again.

'I am Jesus. Trust in me and I will help you.'

The voice was the most exquisite I had ever heard, full of love, gentle but strong, and as I heard his words, I had the most extraordinary sensation that all the pain and anger and hatred fermenting inside me were being pulled upwards out of me through the top of my head. I seemed to be floating above the bed, not lying on it. I stared at the figure beside me. I wanted to speak, but couldn't. A great feeling of peace and warmth crept over me, as though I was being wrapped in a soft cocoon. I felt my eyes begin to close and for the first time in what seemed like years I fell into a dreamless sleep.

II

Aftermath

How does one convey a direct experience of God to another person? I knew that of all the people in the world, Sally would be able to understand and appreciate what had happened to me that night, but I found myself quite unable to tell her. Unable, or unwilling, I can't be sure which, but I know that for some time there seemed to be something preventing me from revealing this experience to anyone else, even my wife. Sally could tell that something significant had happened to me, if only because of the transformation from the angry, brooding man of the evening before, and once or twice I caught her looking at me rather quizzically, but the significance, the enormity of what I had experienced left me bereft of words. I knew I hadn't dreamt it; I knew beyond any shadow of doubt that the presence, the person, in my room had been Jesus Christ himself; that the Son of God, in whose existence I had come to believe intellectually, had physically appeared to me and had brought about a miraculous change in my heart.

The feeling of warmth and peace that had enveloped me at Jesus' words remained with me throughout the weeks that followed. All the hate and anger that I had built up in my mind had completely melted away; I still felt wronged and hurt by events and people, but the animosity against Henry had vanished and I was able to set about putting my affairs in order with a clear head and calm mind. It was obvious that I would have to find another job fairly quickly, but I had no stomach at all to get back into the world of broking. Since leaving the Army it had been my dominant interest in business, but I had lost heart when I lost my company. A good friend in London put his office facilities more or less at my disposal and I began to contact employment agencies and generally put out feelers in the City to see what I could find.

Through a contact I met someone who specialised in Names Agencies and he suggested that this would be the ideal area for me to move into. Right at the centre of Lloyd's, the essence, as it were, are the 'Names', the investors who actually provide the backing for the corporation to operate. They are the ones who stand to lose in the event of major claims being made, such as with the loss of aircraft or shipping, and are often well known people with considerable capital to invest, who need to be introduced to the world of Lloyd's and be kept up to date with events by someone who understands the system. That is where the agencies, who work on behalf of Lloyd's syndicates, come in, and I decided that this was the place for me in the future.

A government report had recently been published which highlighted the conflict of interests which arose when brokers were also the owners of underwriting agencies, and were thus in a position to pressurise underwriters into imprudent application of their skills. The report recommended devolution and the Chairman of Lloyd's was preparing a directive on the subject. My new acquaintance in the employment agency advised me that as soon as this directive was given, there would be a major reshuffling of jobs as companies reorganised their affairs, selling either the broking or the underwriting sides of their business.

'Ian,' he said, 'there will be plenty of opportunities then for someone like you. You're an ideal man for the Names Agency business. You have the right background, public school, Sandhurst; the right contacts, plenty of savoir-faire and, most important, you understand Lloyd's. As soon as the Market gets itself sorted out, your name is at the top of my list.'

Although I was not seriously worried about my future career at that time, I did have occasional moments of black despair about the situation, so these words did come as something of a relief to me. In fact, it was more than relief; I was positively cheered at the prospect of bidding goodbye to one area of work which had turned sour and starting again in another which combined the virtues of familiarity and freshness. I left the employment agency in better spirits than I had been for some time. I would take the advice I had been given and not panic.

'Give yourself a chance to get over all this unpleasant-ness,' he had said. 'Take a couple of months break. Have a holiday. We often see men like you, in this very posi-tion, and things do take a bit of getting used to, so we always advise some kind of a rest, just so they can get things into perspective and get ready to start again.'

I was turning over his words in my mind, and forming some ideas, as I turned into Eastcheap. Suddenly a voice broke into my musings and I looked up to find myself face to face with my former manager, Tom Harvey, the man I had fired almost a year before. I greeted him a little awkwardly but Tom seemed quite at ease and suggested going for a cup of coffee together. When the coffee was on the table and the waitress had disappeared, Tom looked at me and smiled.

'You fired the wrong bloke, Ian,' he said. 'I tried to tell you at the time but you were so convinced that Maurice was the blue-eyed boy and I was the villain of the piece that you never gave me a chance. I could have warned you what was in the offing. Maurice was after your job practically from the start. As soon as Henry Cavendish was on hand in the office, Maurice moved in and started his hatchet job on you. You didn't stand a chance.'

I stared at him. Somehow I wasn't really surprised. I remembered Maurice's silence at the Board meeting, how he had refused to back me up in my assurances to Henry. The phone call from Keith was now well and truly corroborated, if such corroboration were needed.

Tom was looking at me over his coffee cup.

'And in case you're wondering how I know all this,' he continued, 'I've made it my business to keep an eye on the old place since I left. Oh I know I was pretty mad at you at the time, but I knew it was Collighan at the back of it all and I was waiting to see exactly what he would do after he got rid of me. I'm going to fix him one day, no matter how long it takes.'

'Well now you know,' I said, with a trace of bitterness in my voice. 'He got rid of me, too. Or hadn't you heard?'

'Yes, I'd heard,' Tom answered, 'and it gives me no satisfaction at all, in case you're thinking otherwise. I'm very, very sorry. We had a good set-up there in the early days, and I wish things hadn't turned out like this for you.'

I knew by Tom's tone and expression that he was speaking sincerely and I was grateful for that. So Maurice had sold me down the river had he? It was too late now for me to do anything about it. I should not have let him feed me all that comforting bunkum about the company's future prospects; I should have checked everything for myself. He must have known the business wasn't going to come in as he had forecast but he had continued to feed me the placebo of his misplaced optimism and half-truths and I, in my naïvete had believed him.

'What is the able Mr Collighan doing now?' I asked. 'I'm assuming you still have your tabs on the place?'

Tom nodded. 'I do indeed, and from what I hear, he's enjoying himself a good deal, doing your former job, playing the Big White Chief.'

I suppose I expected to feel some kind of surge of anger at what I had just been told me, but there was nothing. I had taken in what Tom had said and I believed him, first because he had no reason to lie to me now, and secondly because of what I had previously heard from Keith, but the words had no noticeable effect on me. I felt no tremor in the warm, soft cocoon of tranquillity and security that had been around me since the night of March 8th. I said goodbye to Tom and went home.

I was looking forward, later that week, to a particularly enjoyable meeting of Lutine Lodge when I, as Worshipful Master, would be taking a major role in the installation of my successor. I knew that I could rely on all members of my Mother Lodge to be supportive and sympathetic in my present difficulties and I was overwhelmingly glad of the comradeship of the Lodge. I entered the house feeling more cheerful than I had for some time, but one look at Sally's face told me that something was wrong.

Three years earlier our younger son, William, now six, had been diagnosed as having intermittent hearing loss. Sally had suspected something was amiss, having already seen two babies through the stages of learning to talk and distinguish sounds, and after a series of examinations and tests, William's problem was discovered. This had obviously made his learning very slow and his teachers suspected that in addition, he might also be dyslexic. Coupled with the fact that he was a hyper-active child, this made teaching him a very difficult job indeed, and his headmistress had finally come to the conclusion that his present prep school was no longer able to cope with the situation. Sally had been called to the school to be told of the decision, and was in despair as to where to send William instead.

In a way, it was one decision less for me to make, as I had no money for the next term's fees anyway, and was fast approaching the point when the children's schools would have to be informed of the position. Edward was coming up to the Common Entrance Examination and to my overwhelming relief, his headmaster showed tremendous understanding and suggested he be left where he was for the time being to 'see what happened'. In fact, what did happen is that the school very generously gave Edward a bursary to enable him to complete his final term. The other children, however, were a different matter, and we had to remove them from their school at the end of the term. Louise had already won a scholarship to her senior school, so there was no pressure on her, and Sally said that she would teach the two younger ones at home for the summer term. By the autumn I would be well established in my next job, and our problems would be at an end; life was not really too bad and, of course, I still had Freemasonry.

Looming on the horizon was a major part for me in the Royal Arch. In December I was due to be made Principal Sojourner and I was really enjoying learning the ritual. The experience I had had of meeting God incarnate had served to crystallise all my views of the Deity, and as a result there was a new depth to both my Masonic activity and my church-going. For the first time in my life I had been overcome with the desire to pray, and I borrowed an old prayer-book of Sally's to help me do this. I would repeat the words over and over, especially the Lord's Prayer, finding a meaning and clarity in them that I had never seen before. I looked forward to the church services in a way that I would have thought impossible only a few weeks earlier.

Our local vicar had been marvellous when he had heard

about my problems, and when I at last felt able to speak of my supernatural experience, it was to him and Sally that I relayed it. For Sally it was a real answer to her prayers of the last sixteen years, and Nicholas, our vicar, received what I had to say with his customary gentle understanding. As for myself, now that the gag was off, so to speak, I was full of the wonderful thing that had happened to me. I still couldn't rationalise it; still less could I imagine why it had happened to me, but now that it had, I wanted the whole world to know about it. Poor Sally was continually subjected to my enthusiastic plans to write a book about this incredible experience, a book which would stun and amaze the world. After all, there could not be many people about who had actually had a real miracle in their lives! Sally's response was to drive me, one day, to the Tonbridge Christian Book Centre, and there, to my mixed disappointment and delight, I found innumerable books on this very subject, hundreds of testimonies to the living God! Apparently this same Jesus, whom I had seen with my own eyes in what I believed must be a unique experience, had been met by many people before me. He had healed, just as he had done when he walked on earth; through belief in him, drug addicts and alcoholics had been released from their addictions and hardened criminals had completely turned away from their former lives and begun to serve others; all over the world it seemed that miracles were still happening, just like those recorded in the New Testament.

I read some of the authors avidly, fascinated by their accounts of wonderful supernatural experiences. Catherine Marshall wrote of a major tragedy in her life, through which she had found God, and when I read her testimony, *Meeting God at Every Turn*, I began to realise that so often it is only in times of severe stress and need that God becomes real to us. It was certainly true in my own case that he had made himself known to me at a point when I had ceased to think and behave rationally. Kathryn Kuhlman was another author whom I came across at this time. Her story *I Believe in Miracles* related the most marvellous accounts of God's power at work—things I'd never thought possible were happening today in America and throughout the world.

It was while I was reading books like these, together with novels by Morris West, and Taylor Cauldwell's *Dear and Glorious Physician*, the story of the apostle Luke, that the full reality of what had passed slowly dawned on me. For the first time I began to understand God not as a great Universal Deity to whom I should pay lip service, but a father, a real father who wanted a real relationship with the children whom he had created. Christian testimony books, together with the Hal Lindsey and Gary Allen works, provided my reading matter throughout that summer. I was still very much taken up with the prophetic literature I had acquired and had become totally convinced that a one-world government was being engineered behind the scenes preparatory to a great apocalyptic event.

In May the Chairman of Lloyd's delivered his long-awaited address on the subject of devolution and I waited confidently for the expected job vacancies to occur. Nothing happened. My contact in the employment agency was puzzled but still confident. June arrived and still no opportunities presented themselves. I had now been unemployed for more than three months, and financially was finding the going hard. The Unemployment Benefit Office was contributing to my mortgage repayments and as I had assured the building society that I would soon be returning to full-time employment, they were reasonably happy with the interim arrangement. However, as the summer wore on with no sign of a job, I was obliged to give them an undertaking to put my house on the market in December, unless I was by then able to resume the monthly payments myself. I was now beginning to get a little concerned about the future; friends were optimistic and encouraging, but still the sudden demand for Names Agents which had been anticipated did not occur.

The most immediate concern was the children's education; Sally was coping admirably with the two little ones, taking them off each day when the weather was fine into the nearby fields to give them their lessons in the open air and leave me to my books or to sit in front of the television and bury myself in the excitement of the Los Angeles Olympics. But it was Edward's future which worried me most and the realisation that I could not now afford to send him to the public school I had chosen for him which hit me hardest. The little ones were blissfully unaware of the gravity of the situation. They knew that Daddy had had a lot of trouble to deal with, but seemed very quickly to get used to the idea of my being home most days. Sally often took them to a pleasant spot near the disused railway line and soon they began to identify with the characters in one of their favourite stories—*The Railway Children*. Those children had also had a Daddy who had been in trouble, just like theirs. It was all very interesting and quite exciting really, not going to school but being taught by Mummy with lots of walks and picnics to make lessons more fun. But summer was coming to an end and Sally could not go on teaching them indefinitely. We enrolled them at a local village school and Edward entered grammar school at the same time. Only Louise, by virtue of her scholarship, began the autumn term in the school she had expected to go to.

By this time I was beginning to feel like some sort of commercial pariah. Whatever avenue I approached seemed to lead nowhere. However helpful friends might wish to be, they still could not come up with anything definite, and slowly but surely the world of business began to seem distant and foreign to me. Six months is a long time to be away from the City and I was losing contact with the world I had previously known so well. All this time it was Freemasonry which kept me sane. At the meetings I had attended, both in my Mother Lodge and in all the different orders to which I belonged, all my brother-Masons had shown me tremendous support and sympathy. During the summer I concentrated on learning my parts for the forthcoming year and I looked forward eagerly to the resumption of meetings in the autumn. Quite apart from the ceremonial side, the social contact kept me feeling human and less like some sort of leper, which I had begun to feel after seeing a former acquaintance, to whom I had given a great deal of premium income, actually cross the street to avoid me!

Then something happened which was to have very far-reaching effects on our lives: Billy Graham arrived in Britain for another evangelistic crusade. When we heard that one of his meetings was to be televised, Sally asked me to video-record it so that she could watch it in peace when the children were safely asleep. I was absolutely riveted by what I saw and heard. I had heard a little of this kind of preaching before and usually regarded it as so much hog-wash, but as I listened to this man speak about the gospel of Jesus Christ and what it meant for twentieth-century man, the whole message came alive and the real meaning of the 'Good News' dawned on me. Suddenly I wanted to read the Bible for myself, something which I had not hitherto felt necessary despite my encounter with its Author! The words which I had heard often enough in church took on new significance and my attitude to them changed; they became what they had never before been to me—the true words of God.

My recording of Billy Graham did much more for me than awaken my interest in the Bible, wonderful though that was; it led me directly to the place where God wanted me to be so he could continue to reveal himself to me.

This came about through our attending the local parish church, St Dunstan's, where the services now gave me a great deal of satisfaction. I had really begun to feel that I was meeting God there, and the taking of the sacraments became the focal point for me. Nicholas, our vicar, continued to take an interest in my newly found relationship with God and each time we met would question me gently as to how I was faring both materially and spiritually. Waiting in the usual queue to say goodbye to him at the end of a Sunday morning service I heard a lady in front of me bemoaning the fact that she had missed the Billy Graham programme, and asking Nicholas if he knew anyone who had recorded it. I hesitated a moment but when I heard Nicholas reply in the negative, I leaned forward to tell her that we had the recording at home. She spun round immediately and asked if she might borrow it. Something prompted me to say, 'No, but you can come and watch it at our house if you would like to.'

That was the start of my acquaintance with Betty Barefield and her husband Keith. A short time later Betty rang and arranged a time to come to see the video and asked if they might bring what she referred to as 'our fellowship group' with them. A week later, Sally and I found ourselves sitting in our drawing room surrounded by a group of total strangers ready to watch the film.

The evening began with a surprise, as Keith began to pray—and such praying! He actually spoke as though God were there in the room with us. He thanked him for the joy of meeting together, asked for a blessing for me for allowing them to come to my home, and chatted to God in the most relaxed way imaginable even while displaying reverence for him. I was rather taken aback by all this informality, and still more so by the running commentary which accompanied the showing of the film.

'Hallelujah!' said one. 'Praise the Lord!' said another. Various exclamations of pleased approval punctuated

Billy Graham's address all uttered freely and spontaneously by my visitors. I was intrigued by them, and so was Sally. We wanted to know more. Who were they? Did they go to church? We had seen only Betty and Keith at St. Dunstan's; where did the others worship? What we noticed most was the real feeling of love which emanated from them. One of the women, who was introduced to us as Eironwy, had obviously suffered a recent trauma, and the other members of the group seemed to be loving her through it—that is really the only way I can describe the caring attitudes I witnessed that evening.

Over coffee and biscuits later, we learned more about our new friends, for we did feel a great friendship almost immediately. We found that Keith was part of a group which organised regular Christian meetings in Tunbridge Wells, only a few miles away. These were entitled 'Come Bless the Lord', and took place at monthly intervals, usually at one or other of the various churches in the town. He and Betty also held regular Thursday evening Bible studies in their home in Mayfield and, as a result of our meeting, Betty invited me to come along to one of them.

I don't know quite what I expected as I entered the pretty beamed cottage which was their home, but what did take place was quite unlike anything I'd known before. In the same relaxed manner as in our home, Keith committed the evening to God and then the singing began. There was no accompaniment at all, just voices raised unself-consciously in praise to the Lord. But the things they sang! No hymns as I understood them, instead rather swingy and catchy tunes which reminded me of folk or country music. After the initial surprise, I must say that I rather enjoyed listening to them, and the enjoyment was greater for the joy I could see on the faces of the singers. No bent heads staring at hymn-books but faces raised and happy expressions all round. When it was time for the

Bible study I listened intently to Keith, first reading a passage of Scripture and then speaking on it with a quiet authority which captured my attention and held it fast. The whole evening was a novel and intriguing experience. The people there covered a wide age range and came from a variety of religious backgrounds, some Catholic, some Protestant, while Keith and Betty themselves had grown up in the Plymouth Brethren. All were now one, it seemed to me, in their love of God.

That evening was the first of many spent at the Barefields' home in praise of God and study of the Bible. In December Betty invited me to accompany them to a 'Come Bless the Lord' meeting. I accepted her invitation a little half-heartedly. I liked all the people I had met very much, and was quite interested in becoming more involved with them, but at that time I was giving almost all my attention to my Masonic activity. Hardly a week went by at this time of year without my attending a gathering of one order or another, and at the December meeting of the Royal Arch I was due to be made Principal Sojourner— something which fulfilled a minor ambition and which would require a great deal of participation for me in future ceremonies. My attitude to Freemasonry was now a little ambivalent. Before my experience of 8th and 9th March, I had been convinced that Freemasonry had all the answers and was streets ahead of the church in the matter of scriptural truth. Since meeting Jesus I now felt a little further on in my quest, as though I had somehow taken a short-cut to God and was now in a privileged position. Freemasonry, however, as far as I was concerned, still held all the answers even if I was happy to go along with these new Christians I had met and see where it would lead.

The December 'Come Bless the Lord' meeting was to be held at the Boys' Grammar School in Tunbridge Wells, and I duly accompanied Betty, Keith and several of their friends to hear the Reverend Edmund Heddle speak on the subject of 'The Fruit of the Spirit'. I took my seat next to Betty, not far from the front of the hall, and the praise and worship began. Suddenly, a movement in the rows in front of me caught my eye, and to my great astonishment I saw the people there raising their hands above their heads as they sang. I turned towards Betty to make some comment under my breath, and saw in horror that she was going the same thing! I was busy wondering what on earth I had got myself into when the greatest shock of all came; the song being sung had a catchy tune and a strong rhythmic beat and in the aisle to my left people started to dance. Individually, they were rocking or jumping about, quite unself-conscious and apparently oblivious to anyone else. Almost unable to believe my own eyes I turned to Betty in scandalised amazement. She, as I later discovered, was fervently praying that this, my first experience of what Christians rather disrespectfully term the 'charismatic bop', would not come as a permanent culture shock to my system!

The pace finally slowed down as we came to a time of prayer; this at least was more dignified than the unrestrained exuberance I had just witnessed, but again I was surprised by the unstructured, almost casual form that the praying took. The sincerity, however, was unmistakable and I wondered, as I prepared to listen to the address, if I would ever be able, or even want, to talk in that way to Almighty God.

Edmund Heddle spoke for almost an hour on the Fruit of the Spirit. The subject matter was unfamiliar to me, but most of his audience seemed to understand exactly what he was talking about and remained wholly attentive throughout. This in itself was a revelation to me—how anyone could happily listen for that length of time to an exposition of the Scriptures. Our much-loved vicar prided himself on the short, punchy message, delivered in a maximum time of eight minutes flat.

It was little more than ten o'clock when I arrived home, and Sally was still up.

'Well?' she greeted me, 'how was it?'

'Different,' I replied, 'but interesting. Very interesting.'

12

No Danger—God at Work!

Despite everything, we had a good Christmas. I was determined that, whatever came or went, the children would enjoy the kind of celebration they had always had. I had no idea what the New Year would bring but Christmas was going to be everything it ought to be, everything it had always been for the family.

With January, reality returned, and I was forced to admit that I was no longer likely to find my way back into the City. I had been pinning my hopes on November as the time when the openings would occur, but when that came and went with nothing for me, my spirits began to sink ever lower, and for the first time the awful fear that I might be totally unemployable crept into my mind.

I was reading one of Catherine Marshall's books when one of the scriptures which she quoted seemed suddenly to become very relevant to me. I turned to my Bible and read it for myself in the Book of Proverbs: 'Trust in the Lord with all your heart. Never rely on what you think you know. Remember the Lord in everything you do, and he will show you the right way. Never let yourself think that you are wiser than you are; simply obey the Lord and refuse to do wrong' (Prov 3:5–7 Good News Bible). For the first time since that momentous night in March, I really began to understand what that meeting meant, what the purpose was behind the revelation of the risen Christ that I received. I knew that Jesus must have picked that moment to enter my life in order to prevent me from committing a terrible sin, but when I read that scripture the full meaning of the words he had used came back to me. Jesus had said, 'Trust in me and I will help you.' I had basked in the peace and warmth which his presence had brought me but I had not taken proper account of his actual words. I had not trusted in him; I was still worrying about the future, worrying more and more, in fact, as time went by. Now God was speaking to me again, repeating exactly the same instruction: I was to trust in him for help and not rely on my own abilities.

This was how I began to learn that God continues to communicate with his children today, not just in the very dramatic way that I had experienced, but through his written word, the Bible, and through other Christians. He used Catherine Marshall again at this time by causing my mind to dwell at great length on a passage in one of her books which talks about a journey. As I lay in bed one night thinking about this, I felt the Lord speaking to me again. I use the word 'felt' rather than 'heard' because this time I was not conscious of any real sound; instead it was a strange sensation that deep inside my body, somewhere in the region of my diaphragm, words were being given to me. The Lord was inviting me to go on a journey with him to a feast he had prepared and I knew he was telling me that at any time I chose I could break the journey if I wanted to stop off and eat elsewhere, but he was going on and if I chose to stay with him there would be a sumptuous banquet at the end.

I desperately wanted to go on that journey with God, not to be left behind by him, and I responded to his words with a promise that I would follow him wherever he led. By way of reassurance the Lord drew my attention, the following day, to two Psalms, 34 and 37, and I found a tremendous comfort in the promises I read there.

Towards the end of January, Betty and Keith invited me to another 'Come Bless the Lord' meeting, as it was by then apparent to them that the somewhat unorthodox behaviour I had observed at the last one had not done me any significant harm. Roger Price was speaking on 'The Gifts of the Spirit', and I was profoundly affected by both the speaker and the message. I was intrigued by something which Roger referred to as 'baptism in the Holy Spirit'. Edmund Heddle had spoken about this, but I can't say that I had understood much on that occasion, but now I began to see the significance of it and its desirability for a Christian.

Interested though I was in the proceedings of the evening, I could not escape the fact that after about the first half-hour I was desperate for a smoke. At that time I was smoking as heavily as I had ever done. It was one of the things I was using as a prop as I saw my world disintegrating around me, but of course, I would not admit that to myself; I regarded it merely as something which I enjoyed and saw no reason to dispense with. At the end of the meeting I made as much haste as was decently possible to get outside and light my pipe. I was enjoying a peaceful few minutes of indulgence when I noticed something going on nearby in the car park. It was a bitterly cold night and all the cars had a good coating of frost. Two young women who had parked their car near Keith's were obviously having trouble getting the key into the frozen lock and as the rest of our group arrived, we all proffered various helpful comments but to no avail. The lock was frozen solid and refused to yield even to a hefty squirt of de-icer which someone produced. Then Keith took charge, and to my astonishment suggested that we all lay hands on the car and pray! Everyone concurred very readily, and I added my hands to theirs, feeling not a little embarrassed. Keith addressed God in his usual easy way, reminding him that we had all been about his business that evening, that we had been listening to one of his servants expounding his word, and now there was a problem hindering the safe return home of two of his children. Would God please free the lock of the car door? We all duly added 'Amen' to Keith's words, and the owner of the car tried again. The key slid into the lock without a sound. I was the only one who looked surprised. That was my first ever experience of answered prayer, and immediate answer into the bargain. Keith smiled at my expression.

'The Lord is there to help us in everything, Ian,' he said gently. I could hardly argue with that now. He seemed to want to be involved in every detail of our daily lives.

Meanwhile, I was determined to learn more about the topic that had so caught my imagination in the last two meetings. When I had coffee with Betty and Keith shortly afterwards, I took the bull by the horns, as it were, and asked them directly how I should go about being baptised in the Holy Spirit. They carefully explained to me that it was something which was available to every Christian through prayer, and then laid hands on me and prayed for me then and there to receive this gift. As Betty and Keith prayed, I had a sensation of lightness and great joy sweeping over me; without realising it I slipped from a standing position onto the sofa behind me, and I felt a great peace and happiness inside, something akin to what I had felt on the night the Lord came to me. The next morning I awoke to find myself praying aloud, just as though I had come to in the middle of a conversation, and for the first time I knew the great happiness of speaking spontaneously to God, of talking to him as a child to a father, instead of using the formal, rather detached method of approach that I had had before.

Roger Price's talk had stirred me more than anything I had heard and it evoked in me an almost passionate desire to read the Bible, which had taken on a whole new relevance and significance for me. Betty introduced me to Roger's marvellous tape ministry and I began collecting his Basic Bible Studies and Special Topic tapes, particularly those on 'Guidance'. I felt very much in need of guidance at this time; on the one hand a whole new world of incredible adventure seemed to be opening up in front of me, while on the other every security I had known was vanishing. My house was now up for sale, but there was almost no movement in the property market due to the heavy snows we were struggling with; no one in their right mind would fight their way round rural Sussex in such weather to view houses, so we were forced to sit tight and wait. I was trying to cling on to what God had told me, and to trust in him, but finding it rather difficult. On one particularly desperate evening, when I felt as though I could not cope for one day longer with the uncertainty of my life, I was doing my best to concentrate on the section of the Bible I had chosen to read, the Book of Isaiah, when I felt God prompting me to turn instead to Genesis. Eventually I responded, turned to the opening words of the Bible and began to read. I found that I was being drawn to carry on reading more and more, until I came to the story of Joseph. I knew that, for some reason, the Lord wanted me to read this. As I finished reading I heard God's voice, very clearly, asking me what I had learned from his word. I realised that the lesson he wanted me to learn was one of patience and faith, and when I told him this, peace once again came back into my anxiety-ridden mind.

It would not be truthful to say that I immediately stopped all worry and began exercising patience and faith. I certainly tried hard, but there were times when, like the apostle Peter walking on the water, I would look at the problems around me, instead of at the Lord, and begin to flounder. Then, just as he had done with Peter, the Lord would stretch out his hand and stop me from sinking, and during the weeks and months that followed my baptism in the Spirit I really saw the truth of Keith's words, that God really does want to help us in everything, large and small. We had marvellous evidence of this in two very contrasting areas, the first of which was the question of my addiction to tobacco.

The family had put up with my smoking reasonably tolerantly, apart from the odd grumble about filthy habits, but quite suddenly everyone seemed to react violently against it and every time I lit my friendly old pipe, there would be coughing and choking and a rush to open windows, all of which I found extremely irritating. I put up with this fuss for a time and then an idea flashed into my mind and I asked the Lord if he was telling me, through the children, that he wanted me to stop smoking. Quite clearly, I heard him answer 'Yes'. It was late in the evening and I was almost ready to go to bed, so I enjoyed a last pipe, told the Lord that that was it, and retired, feeling a great sense of satisfaction. By the next morning, however, all this rather self-righteous feeling had evaporated completely and I was longing for a smoke. In my tobacco pouch was just enough for one pipe; it seemed a shame to waste it, so I gave in to my weakness and lit up 'just once more'. Fatal, of course; half-way through the morning I had to drive into the village for more tobacco.

This went on and on for several weeks; every night I would vow I had smoked for the last time, and every morning I would be faced with an irresistible craving, and succumb to my addiction. I wasn't pleased with myself; I knew that God wanted me to break the habit, but I felt powerless to do so. In addition to my lack of will-power, I also clung onto my pipe as one of the few things which hadn't altered in my life. In a strange way, it was a link with the old Ian Gordon, the confident company director, and I was reluctant to let that link go, however irrational.

One day I was walking with Jasper, the family dog, in the fields near home, when a voice spoke directly into my ear, causing me to stop in my tracks. I heard the Lord asking me if I was going to do what I had said, and give up smoking for him.

'Lord, I can't!' I answered, desperately. 'It's all I've got. I've nothing else left.'

The reply came: 'Aren't you forgetting me?' and suddenly the words Jesus had spoken at my bedside came rushing back—'Trust in me and I will help you.'

'Lord,' I said, 'I will give up, because I know that you want me to, and I want to be obedient to you, but I can't do it on my own. You'll have to help me.'

There were no more words in my ear. Jasper and I finished our walk and went home.

Nothing at all happened during the rest of that day, but as I slowly emerged from sleep the next morning, the voice was there again, speaking directly into my left ear.

'Ian,' the Lord said, 'I am releasing you from your slavery to tobacco.'

At these words, I felt an uncanny sensation in my mouth, as though the whole lining were being drawn out. It was not the pleasantest of feelings but when it stopped after a few seconds, my mouth felt unbelievably cleansed, completely fresh and free from that ghastly morning taste which smokers know so well. I heard the Lord's voice again, telling me to let Sally know what he had done. I leaned across and shook her.

'Sally, listen. The Lord has just freed me from my slavery to tobacco.'

'Praise the Lord!' responded Sally sleepily, and turned over.

My craving for tobacco did not return. It was marvellous to be able to taste and smell things properly for the first time since my youth. Friends in London were amazed that I had been able to break the lifelong habit 'just like that' and that I felt no inclination to accept a cigarette even after lunch, always a difficult time before. I told them that I couldn't take the credit, that it was the Lord who had done it for me, but my words seemed to embarrass them, and whether they believed me or not was hard to know. All my old friends and colleagues knew that I had undergone a transformation since leaving the City but they might have found it difficult to believe that the Lord would involve himself in something so apparently trivial as giving up smoking. As for me, the episode was a tremendous lesson in learning something of the nature of God. I realised that when we are confronted with a situation which we find impossible to cope with in our own strength, God is always there to supply that strength and to help us through it. Just as a human father takes an interest in the everyday doings of his children, so God is concerned with his children's lives, and on hand to help with problems, whatever size they might be. My problem with smoking might have seemed small in the light of everything else I had on my plate, but it had assumed mammoth proportions as I struggled to give it up, and God had stepped in to help me out of my difficulties.

It was the timing of this intervention which first planted in my mind the suspicion that God also has a very definite sense of humour, for the day on which it happened was the first day of Lent, otherwise known as Ash Wednesday!

While I was spending all my time in reading the Bible and listening to Bible study tapes, Sally was quietly continuing her walk with God and had joined the House Group at Betty and Keith's home. Although we had read of many miracles in the testimony of some Christian writers, we had not really registered the full implications of this. It was at her first 'Come Bless the Lord' meeting, listening to Trevor and Anne Dearing, that Sally realised what we now had access to in our relationship with God and his Son. The same power which God had used through his Son, was still available to us, through the Holy Spirit; all we had to do was use it.

Our son, William, was badly in need of a miracle at this time, as his hearing problem had shown no signs of improvement and as a result, his learning was greatly impaired. He was easily two years behind his classmates and the frustration he felt showed itself in disruptive behaviour and an excess of nervous energy. Sally had taken a job at his school and could see at first hand the problems that this caused for all concerned, and we knew it would only be a matter of time before we had to face the fact that an ordinary primary school was not the right place for him. Then Sally decided to involve Jesus in William's problem and everything in our group began to pray for his healing. We continued to pray daily, but nothing noticeable happened; no, one had a word of scripture telling us that our prayers had been answered; I had no voices in my ear, or feelings deep inside me. We carried on praying.

Then in March, we went to hear the evangelist Don Double speaking in Tunbridge Wells. Towards the close, anyone who needed prayer was invited to go forward, and Sally left her seat and walked to the front. I could see her being prayed over, then she vanished from my sight. When God sends his Holy Spirit in response to prayer, the power is so intense that we ordinary human beings often fall to the ground under it. This is what had happened to me, in a very mild way, when I received my baptism in the Spirit, and now it had happened, much more dramatically, to Sally. When she eventually returned to her seat I could see that she had had a marvellous experience; her face shone, and there was a great sense of happiness emanating from her. What I didn't know till later, was that during her time under the influence of the Spirit, she had felt an assurance that our prayers for William had been answered and that he was healed. We actually had to wait for the physical manifestation of this until a few weeks later, when his hearing was tested yet one more time at school. To the astonishment of the medical people, William's hearing had gone suddenly from being very much impaired to being completely normal. They checked the machine; it must be faulty. The machine was fine; they checked William again; the same result. They were incredulous, but William's headmistress, who knew our situation and all the prayers that had been said for him, was overjoyed, and rushed to tell Sally what had happened.

From then on, the difference in William was remarkable; slowly, painfully slowly, he began to progress academically and as he was able to learn properly for the first time, his behaviour improved and he generally started to calm down. Both Sally and his teachers now found him much easier to deal with, and we were freed from the worry of having to find a special school for him. As we got used to the fact that he was now hearing us clearly, we realised just how wonderfully generous the Lord is towards his children, for, not only had he restored William's hearing, but he had given him super-hearing, that is very much more acute than normal. The Lord certainly does not do things by halves!

I was gradually learning to obey Jesus' words, and to trust in him; I had seen the Lord's power at work in our lives, and was spending less time agonising about the future, but then something happened to throw me into a panic once more. My house had been up for sale for several months and so far no one had shown any interest. The local office of the Mortgage Company had been very understanding; the whole of the property market in the area was very sluggish, largely due to the dreadful weather, and they saw no reason to worry unduly. However, Head Office saw things differently. I opened my mail one morning to find a summons to the local Magistrates' Court; they were applying to re-possess my house. I was relying on using the money I would have left from the sale to live on, and if the Mortgagors took possession we would have nowhere to live in the interim. I was sick with anxiety as I arrived with my solicitor at the Court on the appointed day. I didn't know what on earth I could do or say that would persuade the Mortgage Company to give me more time to find a buyer, and in any case, it was probably too late to say anything now that they had chosen to go to law.

We took our places in the courtroom. The solicitor representing the Company was occupied with an enormous file, in which, I reflected glumly, were probably all my letters of excuse and explanation, and requests for more time. I closed my eyes briefly and said, desperately, 'Lord. Please help me.'

The case proceeded. Both solicitors explained the circumstances which had brought the case to court, mine dwelling on the fact that I had undertaken to sell the house, that it had been on the market since December and that the estate agents were optimistic that a buyer would be forthcoming as soon as the weather improved and people began looking at property again. Even as I listened to him I felt as though it was hopeless; the Mortgagors had a point, in that I had now been unemployed for over a year, and they wanted to be sure of their money. If only a buyer had come along!

The Registrar had listened closely to both parties, and now he turned to the 'opposition' and asked to see the agreement which I had signed with them when I took out the mortgage. My heart sank even further. He obviously was not at all swayed by my solicitor's pleas on my behalf, and as soon as these formalities were over he was bound to agree to the re-possession. The solicitor was searching through the file for the necessary document. The Registrar was waiting. The solicitor looked up from the pile of papers and shook his head.

'I'm sorry, sir,' he said, in a puzzled tone. 'The document you require does not appear to be here at the moment.'

The Registrar paused briefly and then addressed both solicitors. To my utter amazement I heard him adjourn the case for two months! My solicitor turned to me with a look of incredulity on his face; neither of us could really believe what had happened. I had two more months in which to sell; we were not going to be made homeless! The relief was overwhelming and all I could say deep in my heart was 'Thank you, thank you, thank you, Lord!'

13

As we forgive those...

Almost since that first evening when we had watched the
Billy Graham video together, Keith and Betty Barefield
had been more or less in the position of my spiritual
mentors. Not only did I benefit a great deal from the
Thursday evening study-groups, but it was through them
that we had been introduced to the 'Come Bless the Lord'
meetings, and thus were able to hear speakers of the
calibre of Edmund Heddle, Roger Price, Trevor Dearing,
Ian Andrews and Americans such as Dan Snead and Jim
Ripley. I was receiving teaching such as I had never
known before. I began sending for tapes of their talks, and
soon had a large collection on a wide variety of Bible
topics. The Chichester Christian Fellowship issues many
basic study tapes free of charge to those with limited
means, and with those I obtained myself, plus tapes lent
me by friends, I think I must have listened to nearly two
hundred in the first six months of 1985. I also got tremendous help from a wonderful little publication called *Every
Day with Jesus*, a study aid which gives readings for each
day, with a commentary by Selwyn Hughes.

For the first time I was receiving Bible teaching from
true believers, men who believed implicitly in the Bible as
the inspired and infallible word of God, and I found the

experience both fascinating and exhilarating. I began to appreciate the coherence of the Bible as the speaker went from one end of it to another in the space of an hour, linking scriptures, illustrating their relevance to each other and to his topic. I saw things I had never seen before, understood passages which had previously made very little sense. There was no 'liberal theology' here, no half-apologies for 'difficult' sections and no dismissal of incidents as merely allegorical. The Scriptures were interpreted clearly and concisely, with continual evidence to support the explanations. I was full of admiration at the depth of Bible knowledge that all the speakers displayed and impressed with their obvious love of the Scriptures.

As my own knowledge increased, with my daily study, Betty and Keith were loving guides and supporters. Both Sally and I felt that we had become very much a part of their fellowship, and the Thursday evening meetings at their home were the highlight of our week. As well as seeing them both on those occasions, we often used to call on Betty for coffee, either individually or together, during the week when the children were at school.

One morning I was enjoying a chat with Betty and, for no reason that I can recall, the subject of Freemasonry came up. The meeting of the Royal Arch for which I had been preparing so conscientiously was shortly to take place; I had learned my part of Principle Sojourner, a major one in the ceremony, with great care and I was really looking forward to the evening, so I was dismayed when Betty challenged me about my activities. She advised me in a gentle but very positive way that Freemasonry was totally incompatible with Christianity, and that I really ought to consider my position in the light of my new relationship with Jesus Christ.

I was disconcerted by Betty's views, views which were shared by Keith, as I discovered when he broached the subject the following Sunday as we were leaving church. I knew both Keith and Betty to be Bible-believing Christians and it bothered me that they should be so misguided about something which was such a major part of my life. As far as I was concerned, Freemasonry had been instrumental in bringing me to a closer understanding of God. The Craft degrees were soundly based on Old Testament scripture, and the Christian orders which I had gone on to join, were the natural extension. How could anyone who was not involved possibly know what they were talking about? And what about the relationship I now had with God, in which he spoke directly to me? Surely if he was not pleased with my masonic activity, he would have told me? He had, after all, spoken to me on quite a number of other subjects!

Quite apart from any religious dimension, Masonry had been a sort of life-line for me since the collapse of my business, and my brother-masons had done much in supporting and encouraging me. In the City, where I had previously felt quite at home, I now felt totally unwelcome. I had become an embarrassment to former friends and colleagues and, with two notable exceptions whose loyalty remained steadfast, I avoided them, feeling that I had become a commercial and social pariah. At Masonic gatherings, however, it was very different; there, I could hold my head up and take my place with confidence. I knew that I fulfilled my roles well; the love of ritual which had begun in school remained with me and demonstrated itself in my approach to meetings, which I took very seriously. Afterwards there was always the pleasure of a first-class dinner in excellent company. These Masonic evenings helped me to feel human again, and my participation in the ceremonies gave me the sense of being needed and important.

I was determined to give a good account of myself as Principal Sojourner. For nine months I had been memorising the part and when the time came, I was word-perfect. The evening went like a dream and my satisfaction was complete when another member of the Chapter, a High Court judge no less, made a point of coming over to speak to me.

'Ian,' he said, 'you really are to be congratulated. That was marvellous. You really made the whole ceremony come alive for us tonight.'

I was elated by this praise; the knowledge that I could still do something well, despite my lack of success in finding a job, did wonders for my sagging morale. I had a splendid evening and wondered how anyone could find anything wrong in this happy, mutually supportive fraternity. There was so much good in Freemasonry, it seemed to me; not just this kind of getting-together and supporting each other, but also a real philanthropy which showed itself in the generous charitable works. Surely that was in keeping with the teachings of Christ himself!

My own, newly-found personal relationship with God had heightened my appreciation of all Masonic ceremonies and each meeting was a source of great satisfaction and reassurance for me. Without this regular association—and I was by now attending about thirty meetings a year in the various orders—I felt there would be a tremendous void in my already much-altered life.

As to how that life was going to turn out, I didn't dare think. Each time I tried to picture the future, I saw nothing. I could not imagine how I was ever going to be able to resume any kind of 'normal' life, such as I had had before. I had heard the Lord telling me to trust him, to have patience and faith, but my acquaintance with him was in its early stages and, like a child, I often felt insecure and needed constant reassurance that everything would be all right. The Lord, like the loving father he is, kept on giving me this reassurance.

One morning in April I was immersed in the Bible when I experienced a completely new phenomenon. I was reading the Book of Isaiah when suddenly my eyes began to play me tricks, or so I thought. The letters on the page in front of me became very indistinct and haphazard, just like a collection of ants let loose on a sheet of paper. All except four lines; these, by contrast, seemed to stand out in sharp relief, completely alone in the midst of all the hieroglyphics, and I read (from Isaiah 61:7):

> Your shame and disgrace are ended.
> You will live in your own land,
> and your wealth will be doubled;
> Your joy will last forever. [Good News Bible]

I knew that, because of the way it had happened, this had to be a word from the Lord, but, perhaps because I was in particularly low spirits that day, or perhaps my faith was lacking, I did not receive them as I should. I laughed what might be termed a rather hollow laugh, and spoke to God in reply.

'Lord,' I said, 'are you joking? Look at me. I'm about to lose my house; I have no prospect of any work; I'm a commercial outcast. What do you mean?'

I heard no response, but three days later I was again reading Isaiah when the same strange phenomenon happened again. This time I read (from Isaiah 55:8, 9):

> "My thoughts," says the Lord, "are not like yours.
> And my ways are different from yours.
> As high as the heavens are above the earth,
> So high are my ways and thoughts above yours."

I had no idea what this phenomenon that I had experienced meant, but I was filled with a tremendous sensation of relief after this second one. I knew the Lord was telling me to stop worrying about the future because he had everything under control and for the first time I really started to relax. I still hadn't sold the house, and I would have to go to court again soon; I still had no prospect of a job; I couldn't see a future ahead of me at all, but I now knew, and really believed, that God was truly in control of the situation and that he would not let me down.

We visited Keith and Betty later that week and I described to her the strange thing that had happened while I was reading. She smiled and looked knowledgeable.

'You've had a rhema,' she said.

'A what?' It sounded as though I'd caught something rather nasty!

'A rhema. It's from the Greek, and it means word. You've had a word from God. It's another way he has of communicating with us.'

I was thrilled, and elated by this confirmation. The Lord was going to restore all my wealth, double it in fact. My goodness, was I going to be wealthy! I could stop worrying from this moment on and leave everything to him.

So much had my faith in the Lord grown, that when I was faced with another Court appearance, two months after the adjournment, I was able to ask him with total confidence to help us again. By this time the house had begun to feel like a millstone round my neck; we had dropped the price to attract a buyer, but still nothing and once again the Mortgage Company were pressing. The same Registrar was presiding, but a different solicitor appeared for the Mortgagors. The case proceeded as before; the document that had been mysteriously missing was produced and the Registrar began to look through all the papers. I held my breath. Suddenly he looked up.

'There seems to be a discrepancy here,' he said. I sat up and watched the two of them examining the paper in the Registrar's hand. After a lot of muttering, the solicitor agreed that there was in fact a discrepancy of two pence in the figures, and she offered to make the necessary alteration. The Registrar demurred.

'I think perhaps not,' he said. 'This admittedly is a very

small amount, but there may well be other errors of a more sizeable nature, so I think it would be advisable to have another adjournment in order that all the figures may be thoroughly checked. Adjourned for two months.'

The expression on the face of my own solicitor at this point was indescribable, and he accompanied me from the Court in a state of bemusement. I wanted to shout aloud at the goodness of God; at last I was really learning that I could absolutely rely on him, even in the face of seemingly impossible situations. I knew that a buyer would now be found, and sure enough, just a few weeks later, we finally sold the house.

The problem of our accommodation helped me to appreciate something I had read in my studies: that the Lord's timing is always perfect, no matter what we think. My intention was to sell the house and find rented accommodation, but when we first tried, there was absolutely nothing suitable for us, even had a buyer come along at that moment. We felt that the children had had enough disruption so we didn't want to change their schools again, and since becoming involved with the Barefields, we had a strong desire to remain in the fellowship. Sally studied list after list from the agent, to no avail, but as soon as our house was sold, the perfect home for us appeared on the list. Sally went to see it, and as soon as she saw it, she knew that it was for us. To confirm matters, the owner was prepared to let us have it from July, when our own home was sold, rather than August which she had originally stated. It was impossible not to see the Lord's hand in all this, and it was another enormous brick in the tower of faith we were building.

Our new Christian friends had all become very dear to us in a comparatively short time, and their constant support in prayer was a tremendous boost. I never ceased to marvel at the harmony which love for God creates among people of such apparently diverse types. Eironwy, one of those who had come to watch Billy Graham, was an extrovert, rather flamboyant woman, who before meeting the Lord had had a very colourful and often very stormy life. She was thrilled by the fact that the Lord communicated with me in the way he did, and began introducing me to others, as 'the man the Lord speaks to as if he's Abraham', a difficult line to follow if ever there was one! This always amused me at first, but one day I questioned the Lord about it, as I was out walking with Jasper. I asked him why he had chosen to speak to me so clearly and audibly; was I the only person to have this marvellous contact, or did he speak to thousands all over the world in the same manner?

I must confess that I was rather proud of being spoken to directly by God; it gave me a lovely feeling of intimacy with the Creator, and I cherished every occasion on which it happened. This time, however, the Lord's answer to my questioning had a very different effect on me. I heard him say 'Ian, there are two kinds of people to whom I speak aloud; one is like my Abraham, and the other kind is so self-centred, arrogant and stubborn that nothing else gets through. Let me tell you, Ian, that you're no Abraham!'

His words cut deep into me and my pride disintegrated. I felt about as low as the weeds I was treading on. Was that how God saw me? Was I really as awful as he had described? I must be; he knew me better than I knew myself, after all, and I knew that he could read my mind and see every thought. Yet he still loved me and had promised to help me always! As I thought about it, I felt very, very humble and I promised the Lord that I would struggle to become more as he would wish me to be.

There was one area of my life which I knew must be displeasing to God, but it was something which I found difficult to alter. Ever since the night of March 8th and 9th, Henry Cavendish had remained in my mind as the villain of the piece. The murderous hatred I had built up had been melted away by my meeting with Jesus, and there was not even any animosity left. But I still held him responsible for my downfall and I told myself that I would never forgive him.

Since my baptism in the Holy Spirit, my praying had become much deeper, more heartfelt and spontaneous than previously; I loved talking to the Lord, just as I'd heard Keith and the others do in the early days, in a relaxed and intimate way as to a father or friend. However, I still enjoyed addressing God in the beautiful, formal words of the Lord's Prayer, and I would repeat it to myself often during my prayer times. On one occasion I came to the line 'Forgive us our trespasses as we forgive those who trespass against us', when I felt the Lord interrupt me with a question.

'Do you really know what you're asking? You want me to forgive you, but I can't truly forgive you until you first forgive Henry.'

I stopped dead in my tracks. I hadn't consciously thought about Henry for some time, so taken up was I with my Bible study and my growing relationship with God, but now here I was, confronted with my own lack of forgiveness. I felt no inclination whatsoever to forgive the man whom I blamed for my present situation, and I told the Lord this. 'I've lost everything,' I said, 'my company, my work, my money and I'm about to lose this house. I *can't* forgive him.' Even as I spoke, I knew that I was totally wrong in my thinking; I hardly had the right to ask God for forgiveness when I was so obdurate about Henry, but try as I might, I could not summon up one ounce of even the most lukewarm feelings. Then something came into my mind that I had read recently in one of the scores of Christian books that I was devouring daily: 'When you find it impossible to do something, ask the Lord to do it through you; when you can't do something in your own strength, do it in his.' It was like light dawning; just as I had found it impossible to give up smoking and had had to ask the Lord to do it for me, I knew I now had to ask him to forgive Henry when I could not.

I prayed from my heart for God to let his forgiveness flow through me to the man who, in my mind, had wronged me. As I prayed, I felt the love of God pass through me like a current of warm air from the top of my head to the soles of my feet, and I knew that God was taking away all of the wrong feelings that I had towards Henry. The release was incredible. I hadn't realised it, but the hurt I was carrying inside had been like a heavy stone, and now it had been lifted from me. I could not believe how light and carefree I now felt. I began to pray for the man whom not so very long ago I had wanted to destroy, and felt a love for him where before had been hatred. 'Agape'—the pure love of God—had taken over my weak human emotions, and the result was beautiful to experience.

In all the anger and resentment that I had built up, it was always Henry whom I blamed, hardly involving Maurice Collighan at all, although I had learned of his part in the affair from Tom and Keith. It was Henry who bore the brunt of my unreasoning resentment, and now that it had been taken away, the Lord showed me in great depth just how much in error I had been. He reminded me of Henry's generous nature, of the kindness he had always shown me in the past, and the doors he had opened for me in my career. I saw that Henry had had to steel himself to do what he had in getting rid of me. His first responsibility was to protect the jobs of the others and the only way to do this was to relieve the company of the burden of my salary and expenses. I recalled now he had tried to do it gently, by suggesting a buy-out, or a sabbatical. I had obstinately pushed him till his back was against the wall and he had no choices left.

Why, oh why, had I not agreed to let him buy me out? I

would not be in this mess now if my own stupid pride hadn't stood in the way. It was my pride, the Lord showed me, which was at the root of much of my problem, the pride that had let me believe I was indispensable, while at the same time I was making myself completely dispensable. I had been so proud of myself for setting up the company and leaving others to run it. I told myself it was good management, that delegation was the art of good command, but now God showed me otherwise. I had sat back and let things slide instead of taking an active part in the running of the office. I had made it easy for Maurice to fool himself—and me—that all was well, by not doing what I should. I had been so absorbed in my Masonic career that I had spent time on that which I should have spent on my company, and now I only had myself to blame for the outcome.

It was as though I was seeing clearly for the first time; everything that had happened now seemed understandable in the light of what the Lord had revealed to me about myself. I had tried, I claimed, to run my company on Christian principles, but God was not in it, so I had no hope of succeeding. I saw it all so clearly, as though a veil had been lifted, and this sudden clarity, together with the lifting of my burden of unforgiveness, induced in me a state of euphoria which lasted for many days.

The Lord, however, had not yet finished with me in the question of forgiveness. He had drawn to my attention the truth behind the words we say so often rather glibly. Forgiveness of sin is a central doctrine of the Christian faith, and the great fundamental difference between it and other religions. God had told me that he could not answer my request for forgiveness unless I forgave Henry; now that I had, through his strength rather than my own, he was about to forgive me my trespasses. I had already realised that God does not do things by halves, but I could not have guessed just how thoroughly he would deal with me.

For about three weeks the Lord prompted me, every day, to lie down on my bed, and close my eyes. I felt no inclination to sleep, no drowsiness came over me, but instead I saw a blank screen in my mind and onto the screen came scenes from my life. I saw and heard incidents which I would have preferred to forget, and had pushed to the back of my mind; people I had hurt, knowingly or otherwise; things I had said and done which were wrong. As each incident appeared on the screen I asked God to forgive me for the sin I had committed, and I truly repented. Day after day this went on; more and more of my past life was recalled to me, and after each 'session' I would open my eyes to find that they were so full of tears that it was like looking through a waterfall. I was not conscious of weeping, but my face and the place where I had been lying were as wet as if I had turned a tap on over myself. I felt as though I had had a refreshing bath or shower, clean and new; it was a very pleasant feeling indeed, and I began to look forward every day to another time of repentance, forgiveness and the joy it was bringing me.

I was in the middle of one of these experiences, when suddenly the picture disappeared and I saw instead one of an enormous book. It was a huge thing, leather-bound, just like one of the great monastic tomes of the middle-ages, and it was full of writing, all about me. It slowly closed and I knew that I was seeing my old life finish. In its place came a modern volume, rather like a desk diary. It opened slowly at the first page, which was empty and a beautiful virgin-white. I then knew with a total certainty that every one of my past sins had been forgiven by God, in his great and limitless mercy, and that I was starting again with a clean sheet.

14

Death of a Passion

Keith and Betty Barefield had disturbed me by their comments on Freemasonry and, fond though I had become of them, I was annoyed that they should seem so opposed to something of which they could only know a tiny part. I had no intention of breaking the vows of secrecy which I had taken, but I sometimes wished I could go into more detail about Masonic ritual and explain it all to them, as it had been explained to me.

At the end of May we were invited to their home to meet a friend of theirs, an Australian priest named Tom Jewett. He gave a talk to our little group in which he discussed the occult, and suddenly Freemasonry was mentioned. 'Oh, no!' I groaned, inwardly. 'Not another of them! However lovely these people are, I do wish they wouldn't go on about something they know nothing about.'

Tom was as condemnatory about the subject as Betty and Keith had been, and a lot more forthright! I felt I just had to tackle him about it and I proceeded to regale him with a spirited defence of the movement, pointing out the good works which it was renowned for, and telling him of the great fraternal spirit in the organisation. I explained that the Craft degrees were all soundly based on the Old

Testament, and how one had to affirm belief in the Trinity before one could be accepted into a Christian Order. 'And,' I finished, triumphantly, 'you will find that throughout history, many eminent men have been Masons. Even members of the present royal family are members of United Grand Lodge of England.'

I paused for breath and waited for Tom's reaction to this coup de grace. He looked directly at me. 'But do they know Jesus?' he asked.

His words, spoken with such powerful simplicity, seemed to go straight into my spirit. I found myself completely without a reply. I was uncomfortable for the rest of the evening, irritated, disturbed, puzzled. Before we left, Tom took me aside and spoke quietly to me, with the same gentle authority. 'Ian,' he said, 'believe me; if you really know Jesus, he will take you out of Freemasonry within six months.'

I drove home with these words echoing in my ears and struggling with very mixed emotions; mild irritation at being 'got at' again by everyone, especially this new priest, and a grudging respect for the authority with which he spoke. He had been so certain in his prediction; very well, I would wait and see. I believed I did know Jesus, better than most, in fact, having had him appear before me in my own bedroom, and it was perfectly possible that Tom was a little misguided about Masonry, as many people were. Time would show.

Through my contact with the Chichester Christian Fellowship, while collecting their tapes, I had heard about a day's seminar which they were planning to hold in June, with the theme of 'Hail to the Coming King'. The subject excited me and I was looking forward to attending along with the rest of our group. I was still very intrigued by any topic which encompassed the second coming of Christ and the destruction of the present system of things, and although my reading matter was now almost totally Christian, I was still very conscious of everything I had read following my conversations with my brother. I was now fully convinced of two things; firstly, that through the development of various 'secret' societies or movements over the past centuries, world governments were now being manipulated by bodies of men whose existence remained totally unknown to the population at large. I recalled a quotation from Benjamin Disraeli: 'the world is governed by very different personages from what is imagined by those who are not behind the scenes', and thought how right he had been in his observation. Secondly I was certain that all this had not happened by chance but had been brought about by the machinations of some malevolent power.

Another statesman, Franklin D Roosevelt once said that nothing in politics happens by accident, and that if anything happened, you could bet it had been planned that way. When I looked at the whole picture of the world which I had formed from all the reading I'd done, that claim made remarkable sense. It was very much like a jigsaw; one piece alone signified nothing, but taken altogether, a very clear and definite picture emerged. I knew now that there was a struggle going on for world domination, and that the person, or being, behind it was Satan. It was he who had prompted the founding of many cults and societies which relied heavily on secrecy to keep their members ignorant of the reality of what was going on. Through the establishment of seemingly unconnected groups, his evil had spread insidiously into innumerable areas, from the blatant devil-worshipping practitioners of the black arts, to the unheard, faceless men of the world of politics, high finance and education.

I could see all this very clearly; what I could not see was how English Freemasonry fitted into it. To me it seemed the direct opposite of anything connected with the devil. I recalled the beauty of the Rose Croix ritual and remembered signing my declaration of faith in the Trinity. Whatever might be happening in the struggle of good against evil, I saw Masonry, embodied by the Rose Croix, as a blazing force on the side of the angels. When the second coming of Christ did eventually take place, this movement, I felt, would surely be vindicated. In the meantime, any teaching or discussion on the subject of the second coming was a source of considerable interest to me.

It was a sunny day in June when we all travelled down to the coast to attend the much-anticipated seminar. A school at Bognor had been borrowed for the day and at lunchtime, after a full and fascinating morning, we all adjourned to the grassed areas outside to enjoy our picnic lunches and to talk over what we had heard. I had finished eating and was debating with myself whether to go and browse around the bookshop or relax a little longer in the sun, when one of our party turned towards me with what I might call a purposeful look on her face.

'Ian', she began, 'you really are going to have to do something about Freemasonry.'

My heart sank. 'Here we go again,' I thought. 'Whose turn is it next?'

Everyone suddenly seemed desperately interested in Freemasonry, or rather, in getting me out of it and after ten minutes or so of reasonably heated discussion, I got to my feet and stomped off, somewhat disgruntled, in the direction of the bookshop. A classroom had been temporarily transformed and there was a good display of reading matter available. 'Here,' I thought, 'at least I'll have a bit of peace and quiet away from all this interminable badgering.' I turned to the nearest stand and the first two books which my gaze fell on were *Christ, the Christian, and Freemasonry* by W J McCormick, and *Should a Christian Be a Mason?* by E M Storms. I stood in front of the stand staring at them. I blinked, but they didn't go away. I stood gazing at them for almost a full minute. I knew why they were there; very hesitantly, almost reluctantly, I picked them both up and bought them.

Those two books dominated my thoughts for the rest of that day, but, strangely enough, I felt as reluctant to open them and read, as I had been to acquire them. When I finally got round to it, a day or so later, what I read, particularly in the Storms book, threw me into a turmoil. I did not finish it. I was torn between dismissing it as irrelevant, as it was concerned with Freemasonry in America, and a sudden, inexplicable feeling that the author might be right. For the first time ever, a terrible suspicion that I was the misguided one came over me; perhaps the division which I had made in my own reasoning, between English Freemasonry and other kinds, was after all totally fallacious, and that all Masonry was one and the same. The thought made me feel quite ill, and over the next few weeks I managed to work myself up into a dreadful state of confusion and uncertainty. Above all, I wanted to obey God and I had been a Christian long enough to know that he often makes his will known to us by means of other Christians; looking back over the past few months I saw how one person after another had brought up the subject of Freemasonry, quite unbidden. Had it been another subject, one on which I was happy to be approached, such as my future work prospects, or the matter of where we were going to live, I would have immediately assumed that the Lord was communicating with me. This was what had happened in the matter of my smoking. Why was I finding it so difficult to accept what was being said to me on the question of my masonic activities?

I had no peace anywhere; I found it impossible to concentrate on anything; my mind was constantly returning to the one burning question: was I wrong about Freemasonry? I went over and over in my mind everything I had done since first joining Lutine Lodge more than

eleven years before. I thought about all the separate rituals of the different Orders which I had joined, and how I
had loved to learn them, and to explain all the intricate
significance to others in their turn. I recalled how my
attitude to Christianity had changed and the great joy and
satisfaction I had experienced in joining the Rose Croix.
Surely that institution could not be contrary to scripture?

Then I remembered the momentary chill I had felt
when I first looked into the chalice of white wine, and my
pulse quickened with fear. When I thought I must go mad
with doubt and uncertainty, the Lord once again spoke. I
heard his words deep inside me telling me to put aside all
my anxious thoughts and let him deal with the problem.
With a great sigh of relief I let go of the tumult in my mind
and once again knew the peace of God.

For some time no one mentioned the subject of Freemasonry. I read nothing about it and heard nothing about
it. We were busy as a family moving from our old home
into the rented house which Sally had been led to in
Mayfield; furniture had to be put into store, specially
prized small items, and the children's toys all taken with
us. I was glad to be leaving the house which I had once
been so proud of acquiring; it had become a source of
worry and anxiety and I was thankful to be rid of it.
Moving into the village would be a lot more convenient all
round, not least in our proximity to church, and to the
Barefield's home, which had become such a focal point for
all of our little Christian group.

Keith had said nothing on the subject of Masonry other
than his original word to me, but one day in the middle of
August he approached me and said, very gently, that he
would like to pray for me with that in mind. I was surprised to find that I was quite happy to agree to this, and
that there was no trace of the irritation which I had always
experienced on previous occasions when the topic came
up. I went to Keith's house and there he prayed that my

eyes would be opened to the truth and that the Lord would direct me in what I must do.

I don't know whether I expected some kind of blinding revelation or other; or perhaps I would once again hear the voice of God clearly. Nothing so dramatic happened. Instead I simply woke up one morning to find that my interest in Freemasonry, and everything connected with it, had died as completely as my longing for tobacco had died that Ash Wednesday morning. I did not feel any animosity, nor any sudden dislike of the movement and its members, rather a complete absence of emotion about the whole thing. After years of being totally engrossed with Freemasonry, almost to the point of obsession, it was a very odd position to find myself in, and I lived for a few days in a sort of state of suspended animation, waiting to discover what would happen next.

When I finally came to the conclusion that I had to resign from Freemasonry, the decision brought with it a great sense of relief that I at last knew what God's will was. I no longer had any doubts; he had told me to leave the matter with him; I had, and he had resolved my problem by simply taking away all desire to remain within the organisation. I thought of Tom Jewett's words to me four months earlier, and now found I could recall them without resentment. He had said that Jesus would bring me out of Freemasonry within six months.

Although I knew what I had to do, I still was not really clear why. I did not have any sudden opening of my eyes, any instant recognition of previously hidden truths, and this puzzled me. Nevertheless, I went ahead with composing my letters of resignation to the Secretaries of the lodges, chapters and preceptories of the six orders and three appendant degrees to which I belonged. This proved a much more difficult task than I had anticipated; time after time I would take out pen and paper, only to get up again from my desk with a sigh of exasperation, and it would be put off till another day. One task, however, I knew I must not shirk; there were two men whom I felt I must tell personally of my decision before I implemented it, one being Hamish Morrison, who had first invited me into the Craft, and had remained a valued friend ever since, and the other a more recent acquaintance who, in the four years I had known him, had shown me tremendous kindness and support, especially in my business troubles. Common courtesy, if nothing else, demanded that these two be given prior notice of the major step I was about to take.

I went first to see Hamish. He was saddened by what I told him; he, like most of my friends and colleagues, knew about my dramatic conversion to Christianity, but he could not follow my reasons for the decision I had reached. His chief concern was that I should not break the vows of secrecy which I had taken, and, even when I explained to him that I could no longer regard these as binding as they had not been taken in the name of the true God, he remained unconvinced. I was sorry that I was causing distress to a man whom I liked and respected, and I was glad that we were able at least to part on good terms.

Gerald, however, was quite another matter. We met for coffee and I told him what I had told Hamish. His reaction was immediate; a look of shocked disbelief came over his face.

'Ian!' he exclaimed. 'How can you possibly contemplate leaving the Brotherhood of Man?'

I looked at him and the words came to me without my being conscious of forming them.

'Because,' I replied, 'it has nothing to do with the family of God.'

At my response, his expression hardened and his eyes went very cold. It was the end of our conversation, and of our friendship. We exchanged desolutory farewells and parted.

Even when you know beyond doubt that you are doing the right thing, it is not always very easy to live with, and I grieved for the loss of a former valued friend. I began to pray for him, and all those others whose eyes, I felt, were closed to the truth, just as mine had been. Even while I was praying, I still was not clear in my own mind about the whys and wherefores of the situation, but the certainty that I was doing God's will did not waver. Finally, on September 10th 1985, I sat down and wrote the letters which had to be written. After more than eleven years of devoted adherence to the movement, I was no longer a Freemason.

15

A Search for the Roots

When my letters of resignation had been finally sealed, stamped and despatched, I experienced a profound sensation of relief and a peace such as I had known only once before—on the night when I met Jesus. For a few days my mind remained tranquil and unconcerned with matters which had been obsessing it for so long, but then my thoughts turned again to the reason why, and I asked God to show me clearly why I had had to renounce Freemasonry.

The way in which he did this once again revealed to me just how perfectly God knows and understands his children. He knew that my faith in the intrinsic purity of the Rose Croix was right at the heart of my Masonic belief; I had come to feel that whatever shortcomings the Craft degrees, and other Orders, might have, the Rose Croix was the essence of pure Christianity. This, if you like, was the cornerstone of my belief, the support on which everything else depended. What follows is an explanation of how God removed that foundational support, how he guided my reading, prompted my memory and opened my eyes to the significance of things I had previously discounted.

I began with the book I had bought three months

earlier—*Should a Christian be a Mason?* by E M Storms. This book carries a foreword written by a former 33rd (and highest) Degree Mason, the Reverend Jim Shaw, and this time I gave it more attention than I had at first reading. On the first page I came across the name of Albert Pike, which immediately rang a bell with me. Where had I encountered this name before? On my bookshelves were all the volumes I had acquired as a result of my discussions with my brother Graham in Australia three years before, and among these was Lady Queenborough's book *Occult Theocrasy*. That was where I had come across Pike.

In an earlier chapter I have said that, following my conversations with Graham, I undertook some research of my own and it is necessary now to give some of the results of that research in order to give the reader a proper perspective. Although I did extensive reading at the time, I did not appreciate the significance of my discoveries until after the Lord had brought me out of Freemasonry and led me into further study. What follows is a necessarily condensed summary of what I have learned, from various sources, and I recommend that anyone interested enough to want further detail should refer to the bibliography at the end of this book.

Freemasonry, which had begun as a society for working masons, much like the guilds of the later Middle Ages, had developed much further over the years than the original three degrees of the Craft, known as 'operative masonry'. Other degrees had emerged, both in England and France, during the eighteenth century, and these developed into what was named 'The Ancient and Accepted Rite'. I myself had progressed to the eighteenth degree when I became a Sovereign Prince of the Rose Croix, and it is in that name that we find an indication of the origin of these extra degrees. The Rosicrucians, or 'Brethren of the Rosy Cross', had begun in Europe as a sect of philosophers who claimed knowledge of all the sciences, chiefly medicine, and many secrets of the universe. These were received by tradition from the Egyptians, Chaldeans and other ancient pagan civilisations. As Europe emerged from the Dark Ages, the unrelenting quest for knowledge and enlightenment spread throughout the continent, and at the close of the sixteenth century many philosophers, alchemists, spiritists and practitioners of astrology had assumed the name of this sect. In October 1617, in Magdeburg, Germany, a meeting was held at which it was formally agreed that the Brotherhood of the Rose Croix must maintain the strictest secrecy for a hundred years. It renewed its oath to destroy the church of Jesus Christ and decreed that in the year 1717 it would transform the fraternity into an association which would carry on a more overt campaign while remaining within the bounds of prudence.

So how did this anti-Christian secret society arrive in England and infiltrate Freemasonry? The quest for knowledge was not restricted to Europe, and alchemists and astrologers played just as large a role in the English court as in the French, German and Swedish. Elizabeth I always considered the advice of her alchemist, one John Dee, in matters affecting national policy, and Dee, in turn, always used his crystal-gazer as a medium. So dabbling in various mystical arts was a commonly accepted practice and any society which encouraged the development of this, particularly within a restricted membership, was almost certain to be welcomed. Robert Fludd, a well-known physician of the time, published in 1617 a treatise in explanation of the Rose Croix. He was greatly helped in the foundation of the Order in England by Francis Bacon, the writer and philosopher. One of those present at the Magdeburg meeting had been an English architect named Nicholas Stone. His interest in the black arts made him a valued and active member of the sect and he composed rituals for the nine grades of the fraternity. As an architect, belonging to the guild of Freemasons, he had assisted Inigo Jones, the Grand Master of the English lodges, which at this period were non-sectarian and had grown from their initial membership of practising masons, to include many who were admitted to the Lodge in an honorary capacity. These 'accepted masons' included peers of the realm, men of letters, professional men and a good number of the wealthy middle class. One such honorary member was Thomas Vaughan, a Rosicrucian, who was impressed and influenced by the writings of Nicholas Stone and saw in the extended membership of the lodges the perfect medium for the propagation of Rosicrucian doctrines.

Thus 'speculative' Masonry, as contrasted with the original 'operative', developed and flourished in England, as on the continent. Then in 1663, at the General Assembly of Masons, the masters of operative Masonry, feeling themselves in very much of a minority, realised that their only way forward, if they did not wish to leave their Lodge, was to unite with their new masters, and fall in with their designs for the future of Freemasonry. Lord St Albans was elected and installed Grand Master, Sir John Denham became his deputy, and Sir Christopher Wren and John Webb, wardens. By the time the English Grand Lodge was founded, on 24th June 1717, significantly one hundred years after the Magdeburg resolution, by James Anderson and six others, including an expatriate Frenchman named Desaguliers who was said to have been head of the Rose Croix, the first three degrees only, Apprentice, Fellow-Craft and Master Mason, were being worked. Shortly after this, although its exact origin has never been totally ascertained, the Royal Arch came into being as a completion of the Third Degree and any who wished to progress to the higher degrees were obliged to enter The

Ancient and Accepted Rite or some other International Order which worked the higher grades.

Until the latter half of the eighteenth century, Freemasonry was confined to Europe, but it soon spread to the New World. In 1761 the Grand Lodge of France, in conjunction with the Council of Knights of the East, deputed a man called Stephen Morin to promulgate Masonry in the West Indies, and it was through his efforts there that Scottish Rite Masonry found its way into America. (The term 'Ecossais' or 'Scottish' had been introduced by the French to distinguish the new degrees from the older English ones.) Although in 1766 Morin's patent was revoked by the Grand Body in Paris for 'propagating strange and mysterious doctrines' he had by then seen the establishment of a 'Sublime Lodge of Perfection' in Boston, in the north, and in fact went on to erect a similar lodge in Charleston, in the south. These two Masonic powers went on to create numerous other lodges throughout America, but because of that country's enormous size, progress was slow. Too slow in fact, for a certain Hyman Isaac Long, who was to play an important role in the development of the Ancient Rite. He was an ambitious man, full of ideas, and frustrated by the slow growth of American Masonry. He left Charleston for Europe where he stayed for the next six years. When he returned, he brought with him his great plan which was the creation of a rite of thirty-three degrees, destined to become universal. Together with other officers of the Lodge, he constituted this rite, taking twenty-five degrees of the system of Heredom (the Rose Croix), six Templar grades, in which were merged four degrees borrowed from the Bavarian Illuminism of Adam Weishaupt, and two grades of administration. He himself took the title of Sovereign Grand Inspector General 33rd and last degree, he gave the institution the name of Ancient and Accepted Scottish

Rite, and the first great constitutions were signed at Charleston, on May 31st 1801.

In 1819 a patent was granted to the Duke of Sussex to form a Supreme Council in England, but it was not acted upon at that time. Finally, in 1845, the Supreme Council for England and Wales was formed and this assumed control of all independent Rose Croix degrees.

This, then, is a condensed history of the supposedly Christian Order, of which I had been so proud, an Order which had its origins in the occultic societies of European Rosicrucianism and Kabbalism (a tradition of Jewish mysticism which I explain more fully in the next chapter). Until the Lord opened my eyes, I have been oblivious to the significance of any of this.

Now, to return to Albert Pike, whose name I had found when I first opened E M Storms' book: Pike had succeeded Isaac Long in 1859 as Sovereign Grand Commander for the Southern Jurisdiction of the United States, having risen rapidly in Freemasonry since his initiation in 1850. He was a great student of the occult and of the Kabbala and author of such works as *Morals and Dogma*, which E M Storms used extensively in researching *Should a Christian be a Mason?* and *The Book of Apadno* which contains the prophecies concerning the reign of the Anti-Christ, from the Satanic point of view. Pike was a self-confessed Luciferian, or Devil-worshipper and was far from alone in his pursuit of the occult; his great friend, Gallatin Mackey, Secretary of the Supreme Council at Charleston, had similar interests, as did Moses Holbrook, Sovereign Grand Commander in 1837.

In 1889, Pike issued 'instructions' to the twenty-three Supreme Councils of the world which reveal his theology beyond any question, part of which ran as follows:

To you, Sovereign Grand Inspectors General, we say this, that you may repeat it to the Brethren of the 32nd, 31st and

30th Degrees—The Masonic religion should be, by all of us initiates of the high degrees, maintained in the purity of the Luciferian doctrine.

Pike goes on to maintain that Lucifer is God, the equal of the Christian God Adonay [sic], and that

the true and pure philosophic religion is the belief in Lucifer, the equal of Adonay; but Lucifer, God of Light and God of Good, is struggling for humanity against Adonay, the God of Darkness and Evil.[1]

When God led me to discover this irrefutable evidence that the Order which I loved more than any other had been presided over by, and received its instructions from a practising Luciferian, my reaction was one of total horror, so much so that I felt physically sick. I had reached the eighteenth degree of the Rose Croix, when I was installed, and had anticipated advancing in the Order as far as I could, continuing to learn more and more of the 'mysteries' as I did so. I had believed them to be deep truths about Christianity; now I realised, with a surge of revulsion, that that was far from being the case.

Then a question flashed into my mind; what about the declaration of faith which I had been required to make, preparatory to entering the Rose Croix? I had had to state, very firmly, my belief in the Trinity. How could I possibly reconcile that with what I now knew? I found the answer in the closing chapter of E M Storms' book, and I reproduce here the Lecture of the 32nd Degree in its entirety, from which the reader will be able to see, as I saw, just how much 'pure Christianity' it embodies. I am indebted to E M Storms for the reproduction of this lecture, as it is to the best of my knowledge still inaccessible in this country to all but those of the 32nd Degree and above. As the Rose Croix in England received its charter from America, it is logical to assume that the ritual is the same in its essentials in both countries. (The emphases are mine.)

We come now to the great symbol of Pythagoras (the Greek philosopher). Our symbols have descended to us from the Aryans, and many were invented by Pythagoras, who studied at Egypt **and Babylon**. In order to preserve the Great Truths from the profane (anyone not a Mason), there were invented some of our symbols that represent the profoundest of truths descended to us from our white ancestors. Many have been lost. Lost, as was the Great Word at the death of Hiram Abiff.

The ancient Masons invented some of these symbols to express the results of their contemplation of deity. They did not attempt to name him, but rather tried to express their reverence by describing him as Ahura-Mazda, spirit of light (Ahura-Mazda is a nature god of Zoroastrianism, a Persian god worshipped with fire).

They conceived the idea that Ahura had seven potencies or emanations. Four of these they thought of as being male and three female. The four male potencies **of Ahura by which he governed the Universe** were: the divine might, the divine wisdom, the divine word and the divine sovereignty. The three female potencies were: productiveness, health and vitality.

Behold in the east, the seven pointed star, the great symbol of this degree, with the seven colours of the rainbow. The seven colours and the seven points represent the seven potencies of Ahura.

Observe now the great delta of Pythagoras consisting of thirty-six lights arranged in eight rows, to form an equilateral triangle. The light at the apex of the delta represents Ahura-Mazda, source of **all light**. This represents the seven remaining potencies of Ahura.

The right angle triangle of three lights around the altar represents the famous forty-seventh proposition of Euclid, or the Pythagorean theorem, which is used to conceal and reveal philosophical truths. **The real significance of the cross** is that of Ahura and his four male emanations, emanating from him. The four animals of the prophet Ezekiel represent these same four male emanations: man, the divine word; the eagle, divine wisdom; the bull, divine might and the lion, divine sovereignty.

Every equilateral triangle **is a symbol of trinity**, as are all groups of three in the lodge, in the sacred and mystic symbol "AUM" of the Hindoos (sic), whose origin and meaning no one here knows. The great trinity of the Aryans was symbolised by the Adepts. Among the Hindoos it symbolised a supreme god of gods. The Brahmins, because of its awful and sacred meaning, hesitated to pronounce it aloud. And when doing so, placed a hand in front of the mouth to deaden the sound. **This trilateral name for god is composed of three sanskrit letters. The first letter "A" stands for the creator (Brahma); the second letter "U" for (Vishnu) the preserver; the third "M" for (Siva) the destroyer.** "AUM", it is ineffable, not because it cannot be pronounced, because it is pronounced A-A-A-U-U-U-M-M-M. All these things which you can learn by study, concentration and contemplation, have come down to us from our ancient ancestors through Zarathrustra and Pythagoras.

You have now reached the mountain peak of Masonic instruction, a peak covered by a mist, which you in search for further light can pierce only by your own efforts. Now we hope you will study diligently the lessons of all our degrees, so that there will be nurtured within you a consuming desire to pierce the pure white light of Masonic wisdom.

And before you go, let me give you a hint; and that is all that the great mystics ever give, as to how you may learn to find that light. The hint is in the Royal Secret, that **true Word**. Man is born with a double nature: what we call good and what we call evil; spiritual and earthly; mortal and immortal. And finds the purpose of his being only when these two natures are in perfect harmony, like the harmonies of the Universe. Harmony, my brethren, harmony is for the **true word** and the Royal Secret which makes possible the empire of true Masonic brotherhood.

I read and re-read this address several times and suddenly saw with total clarity the deception to which I had previously been blind. Not only did all of this flatly contradict Jesus's own teaching that he himself was the Truth (John 14:6) and the Light of the World (John 8:12), but the Trinity referred to by the Rose Croix was not the Christian concept of one God in three persons—Father, Son and Holy Spirit—but instead was something completely un-Christian, that is Brahma, Vishnu and Siva, an unholy trinity of Hindu deities. I was appalled and told myself this could not be, and yet, there it was, in black and white, irrefutable proof that this so-called Christian order of Freemasons bears about as much resemblance to Christianity as day to night. I might never have heard this lecture; very few Masons attain the 32nd Degree, but had I continued in my membership I might have continued for another twenty or more years towards that goal, under a complete delusion. I had gone through the ritual accepting on trust everything I was told, performing the actions required and all the time I was taking part in—what exactly? I had to find out.

On my bookshelves I had a copy of a book published by a firm of Masonic publishers, called *The Genuine Secrets of Freemasonry*, by a Masonic scholar, the Reverend F de P Castells. On the first page I found the clue to what I was seeking:

'We can no longer say,' I read, 'that the origin of Freemasonry is a mystery; the Ritual in our hands is its birth certificate.'

The ritual; that was where the answer lay. I must examine the Rose Croix ritual. I thanked God for his guidance and prayed that he would lead me to see clearly what I needed to see.

I could recall in detail the evening of my 'perfection' into the Rose Croix. I remembered the anticipation, almost excitement, which I had felt as I prepared for the

ceremony, the aesthetic pleasure at the beauty of the
setting and the ritual, and the great sense of satisfaction
when all was over. I had been welcomed by the Sovereign
with the news that Masonry was in a state of despair,
having suffered a grievous loss due to the death of the
Messiah. This now struck me as rather odd, for surely the
whole point of the Messiah's life was that he had to die.
(Luke 18:31–34) The ransom sacrifice of Jesus, the Lamb
of God, (see Matthew 20:28) is central to the Christian
faith, and the fact that he defeated death and opened the
way to eternal life for all believers is a focal point of
Christianity, and a source of rejoicing, not despair. Why
should Masonry be in despair at his death? Who stood to
lose by it? Not Jesus; he rose and triumphed over the
grave. Not mankind; the way back to God was now open
to them. Who, then? There was only one person who lost
out at Calvary, and that was God's old adversary, Satan.
Despite all his efforts, Jesus, the Son of God, had
remained obedient to his Father, and in dying on the
Cross had overcome death, and freed mankind from its
curse, which Satan had brought upon them. If anyone
should despair at the death of the Messiah, it was surely
Satan, the fallen angel, Lucifer himself.

The Rose Croix ritual had consisted of a search for the
lost Word, and I, like so many before me, had happily
embarked upon it without stopping to think that the
Word, the genuine true Word of God, was actually far
from lost. Having become flesh and dwelt amongst men
for thirty-three years, the Word was now seated at the
right hand of God in heaven (see John's Gospel, chapter
1). I had carried out my part in the ceremony, and 'found'
the Word, that is the four letters INRI, Jesus of Nazareth,
King of the Jews, the name of God's son, the Word of
God made flesh; and then what had happened to that
name? In front of the altar I had seen it burned 'to keep it
from the eyes of the profane'; but Jesus' name should

never be kept from anyone, profane or otherwise, for had he not come to save sinners? How could this be done if his name is to be kept from all but a few? As Acts, chapter 4 verse 12 (NIV) tells us 'Salvation is found in no-one else, for there is no other name under heaven given to men by which we must be saved.'

As I thought about this aspect of the ritual, I remembered how I had wished I could share it all with Sally, and how I had pitied others, outside Freemasonry, who were denied access to these secret truths. But Jesus came to bring the truth to all, men, women and children, and instructed his disciples to do the same. 'He said to them, "Go into all the world and preach the good news to all creation" ' (Mark 16:15, NIV). He did not come merely to reveal it piecemeal to exclusive groups of men, bound together by secret vows! Secrets, secrets, secrets everywhere; more secrets to be revealed later, then still more as one moves upwards through the degrees, towards the ultimate 33rd instituted by Isaac Long in 1801.

I finally realised, with total certainty, that the supposedly Christian Order which I had been so anxious to join, had nothing whatsoever to do with Christianity; the constant allusions to Jesus of Nazareth and the apparently Christian symbolism thus rendered it a complete counterfeit and I knew that the inner voice which had cried out in protest at the white wine and salt used in the final part of the ritual had been right.

'You cannot drink the cup of the Lord and the cup of demons too; you cannot have a part in both the Lord's table and the table of demons.' (1 Corinthians 10:21, NIV)

I felt sick. Had I indeed partaken of the table of demons? I recalled my brother's horrified warning that the Rose Croix involved marriage with Satan and how I had dismissed this suggestion as preposterous, but now a faint recollection stirred in the back of my mind. Where had I read something about a marriage? I turned to Keith B

Jackson's *Beyond the Craft*. On the subject of the 33rd Degree of the Rose Croix, that of Sovereign Grand Inspector General, I read the following:

> The supreme degree of the Rite incorporates a most impressive ceremony in which the candidate is required to endure a test demanding great courage, this being followed by a lengthy obligation and fitting climax, **when he is married to the Order with a golden ring of special significance**.

My mind was teeming with questions. Exactly what was the basis of this ritual which had seemed to offer the way to a closer understanding of God but contained nothing of God's truth in it? What lay behind all the teaching, the ritual, the secrecy, the vows? It was not Jesus Christ, but was it really his arch-enemy? I was determined to find out.

Note

[1] Translation from *La Femme et L'Enfant dans la Franc-Maçonnerie Universelle,* by A C De La Rue, p588.

16

The Kabbala

Once I was sure that Freemasonry was not, as I had
believed, based on the Holy Bible, but rather at variance
with it in its essential ritual, I understood why the Bible-
believing Christians I had met had been so concerned with
my adherence to the organisation. I could now see, as they
did, that it is totally impossible for a professing Christian
to reconcile Masonic teaching with Christian doctrine. I
had been completely deluded, and I now began to wonder
just how many others like me were ignorant of the real
secrets which lay behind the seemingly innocuous,
symbol-ridden ceremonies in which they took part. I still
had not answered the question of its real basis, but I was
soon pointed in the right direction by what I read in the
preface to F de P Castell's book *The Genuine Secrets of
Freemasonry*. This Masonic historian says quite definitely
that his book provides 'the final and crowning proof that
Freemasonry is Kabbalism in another garb.' There it was,
straight from the horse's mouth, so to speak. Now all I
had to do was find out exactly what Kabbalism was, and I
would have my answer.

The word 'Kabbala' (also spelt Kabala, Cab[b]ala,
Qab[b]ala) was not entirely unknown to me; I had first
come across it some time earlier in the works of Nesta

Webster and others, and knew it to be some kind of occult mystic Jewish tradition. It was based on a complex numerological system and although I had not really grasped all the finer points, I was nevertheless disturbed enough by its similarity to Masonry in its nomenclature, its symbolism and its progressive development through various stages in a quest for enlightenment, that I had actually mentioned it at one of the meetings of the Rose Croix. I had been told very quickly that the two things were totally different. Looking back, however, I realised that, following my inquiry, my progression in the Rose Croix turned from having been very rapid to almost non-existent. About a year later, after I had continued attending all meetings and taking part in everything as before, I was asked if I had now got things clear in my own mind. When I answered that I had, for I had now almost forgotten about the Kabbala, my 'career' resumed. At the time I made no connection between the events, but now I wondered whether I had been quite deliberately left for a while for the senior members of the Order to ensure that I was still suitable to be allowed to progress further.

The Concise Oxford Dictionary defines 'Cab(b)ala' as 'Jewish oral tradition, mystic interpretation, esoteric doctrine, occult lore'; 'esoteric' as 'meant only for the initiated' and 'occult' as 'kept secret, esoteric, recondite, mysterious, beyond the range of ordinary knowledge, involving the supernatural, mystical, magical.'

I had on my bookshelves a volume called *The Mystical Qabalah* which I had acquired some time earlier from the Theosophical Society's bookshop in London. Written by a practising Kabbalist, Dion Fortune, it carries the following introduction on its jacket:

The Qabalah is the traditional mystical system of Israel. It also formed the basis of mediaeval magic. McGregor Mathers, Wynn Westcott and other modern Qabalists made use of the Tree of Life, the curious diagram which is the key to the practical Qabalah as a system of illuminism.

This book deals with the work of the modern Qabalists as a contribution to the psychology of mystical experience, and also throws much light on the nature of primitive religion and the Mystery Cults.

I knew that Wynn Westcott had held office in the Grand Lodge of England in the early part of this century; in fact he was appointed Junior Grand Deacon in 1902, and was also head of the 'Societas Rosicruciana in Anglia' which of course, still operates as a further Order of Masonry in this country. I had not, until reading Dion Fortune's book, known of him as a practising Kabbalist.

This is not an easy book for the layman to read, dealing as it does with abstract philosophical concepts. I believe firmly that the Lord guided me in my study of this book and enabled me to see clearly, and grasp, the relevant points, and I now propose to try to explain in simple terms what the Kabbala is, where it originated, its relationship if any to the Holy Bible, and its resemblance to Free-masonry.

From time immemorial man has been interested in such questions as his own origins, his psyche, the nature of the universe and of God. In every civilisation there have been the thinkers, the searchers, who were engaged in a constant quest for knowledge and truth, and the mystics whose aim was to achieve union with God. Many were blessed by the discovery of Jesus Christ, who himself was 'the way, the truth and the life' (John 14:6) and before Jesus there were many who knew the true God, and worshipped him alone in a pure and unsullied way. God chose the Jewish race as his own people, and much of their history is recorded in the Old Testament. For those godly men, Jews or Christians, it was a simple matter of knowing God as their father and enjoying a direct relationship with him, as did Abraham, David and all the prophets, followed later by Paul and the Apostles and all those who accepted Jesus as the promised Messiah, God incarnate.

It would seem that the first Kabbalists were not content with such a simple notion of God and employed a complex system of calculation in order to reveal deep spiritual truths. At first only an oral tradition, handed down among the initiates, part of it later became established as the written Kabbala and both written and oral traditions have survived to the present day as a supposed guide to enlightenment for students and practitioners.

The Christian doctrine is straightforward, and simple enough for a child to understand; if we believe in Jesus Christ as the Son of God, who redeemed us from sin, we have eternal life. It is freely available to all, and does not have to be kept secret from all but the initiated, to be explained, little by little, as the seeker moves upward on some kind of ladder. This is basically what the Kabbalist does, and of course the Freemason. Just as the adherent of Freemasonry progresses through the degrees, receiving more instruction at each level of attainment as he moves towards what the 32nd Degree lecture calls 'the pure white light of Masonic wisdom' (see previous chapter), so the student of the Kabbala moves through 'Sephiroth' by way of twenty-two inter-connecting paths of the Tree of Life in his quest for wisdom. This can, according to his philosophy, take many lifetimes, as he constantly under-goes a reincarnation until he reaches his aim of pure union with God, thus becoming part of the supreme Deity himself. Reincarnation has no part in Christian belief; the Epistle to the Hebrews shows it to be totally fallacious: 'Just as man is destined to die once, and after that to face judgment, so Christ was sacrificed once to take away the sins of many people.' (Hebrews 9:27–28)

The Kabbalist uses the diagrammatic tree as an epit-ome of the Macrocosm, that is the universe, and the symbols on it are aimed at putting him in touch with the different spheres of nature. Each Sephirah has its own name, its own position on the Tree of Life, its own attributes and its own symbols. To quote from the Shorter Oxford English Dictionary, 'Sephiroth' is defined thus: 'In the philosophy of the Caballa, the ten hypostatized attributes or emanations by means of which the Infinite enters into relation with the finite.' Put more simply, they are points of understanding where the 'finite', that is man, can grasp more clearly the nature of the infinite Deity, something which has intrigued him for centuries.

Most of us are aware of the innumerable cults and societies which seem to be springing into existence almost daily, as more and more people, particularly the young, become interested in exploring new sensations and trying to discover the meaning of life, the truth about creation and the capacity of the human mind. In the 1960's, Transcendental Meditation became the vogue, and many people in the Western hemisphere adopted the techniques of the Eastern mystics in attempts to raise their minds onto another plane, to achieve a state of exalted consciousness. This is what the Kabbalist is seeking to do as he takes the diagram of the Tree of Life and through study and meditation follows its paths. He is involved in the process of spiritual diagnosis or divination, as he moves in his meditations from one Sephirah to another. Only when he has grasped one does he have the key to the next and so on.

What struck me forcibly as I wrestled with the intricacies of this philosophical system was its bracketing together, metaphorically speaking, of God and Jesus with the deities of all other pantheons, such as Greek and Roman, Hindu etc. The Kabbala claims to be essentially monotheistic, in that it has at its highest point a godhead, that is pure spirit; this is the universal deity which all men worship, and in seeking to attain union with this, any method of divination may be employed, the Egyptian,

Greek, Nordic, Druidic etc. In following his chosen method, the Kabbalist 'encounters' whatever deities are appropriate to his method at each level. Jesus Christ, the Son of God, seems to make an appearance in the sixth Sephirah, named Tiphareth. The 'magical images' ascribed to this point are 'A majestic king; a child; a sacrificed god.' 'Titles' given to it: 'Melekh, the King; Adam; the Son. The Man.' The 'Spiritual experience' connected with it includes 'Mysteries of the Crucifixion' and its symbols 'The Rosy Cross, the Calvary Cross, the truncated pyramid, the cube.'

If some of these notions of symbols and attributes are vaguely familiar to the reader, it is not too surprising, as most of us have come across horoscopes, signs of the zodiac, astrologers (so-called), and can recognise what is meant by the terms. For example, each sign of the zodiac is supposed to dictate human characteristics and to have a 'birthstone'. Have you ever wondered where this and other similar practices which we call occultism originated? After studying the Kabbala even at the level which I did, I am totally certain that it is as Dion Fortune says, 'the fountain-head whence their [the students of occultism] tradition springs' and in 'students of occultism' we include all practitioners of secret or hidden arts, from the alchemists of the middle ages to the practitioners of witchcraft, magic, spiritism and spiritualism, and readers of Tarot cards and casters of horoscopes today. Incidentally, each Sephirah on the Kabbalists' Tree of Life is assigned four Tarot cards, those sinister aids to fortune-telling which have been responsible for leading many gullible people, particularly the young, into situations which they could not control.

Enough of what the Kabbala is; even from this necessarily very basic sketch, I trust the reader will have grasped some idea of what we are dealing with. What is the Christian, or indeed the Jew, to make of it? 'Spiritual diagnosis' or 'divination' which is the aim of the Kabbalist, was expressly forbidden to the Israelites (see Leviticus 19:26, 31, and Deuteronomy 18:10), while in the Acts of the Apostles we read of Paul releasing a slave girl from the power of an evil spirit which had enabled her to tell fortunes (see Acts 16:16–18). There can be no doubt that all meddling with the occult, the hidden things, is displeasing to God; the Bible clearly states that 'the secret things belong to the Lord our God, but the things revealed belong to us and to our children for ever, that we may follow all the words of this law' (Deuteronomy 29:29, NIV). God has revealed what is necessary and beneficial to man, and even such apparently harmless and 'fun' things as horoscopes in newspapers should be viewed in the light of their origins.

I wonder, further, how the Christian is to view the linking of Jesus, who was God incarnate, with the names of heathen gods, as in the following:

> Tiphareth, however, is not only the centre of the Sacrificed God, but also the centre of the Inebriating God, the Giver of Illumination. Dionysos is assigned to this centre as well as Osiris, for, as we have already seen, the Central Pillar is concerned with the modes of consciousness; and human consciousness, rising from Yesod by the Path of the Arrow receives illumination in Tiphareth; therefore all the givers of illumination in the Pantheons are assigned to Tiphareth.

For the Christian there can be no 'giver of illumination' other than Christ himself, 'the true light that gives light to every man coming into the world' (John 1:9). He is the only one who can reveal God to us, and he alone is the path to the Godhead. He came that 'all who believed in him should not perish but have everlasting life' (John 3:16); he constantly testified that he had come from the Father, that who had seen him had also seen the Father

(John 14:9). It is claimed that the Kabbala, the 'mysticism of Israel', is the key to understanding the Bible but, is it logical to suppose that a God who came in human form and taught the poor and uneducated people of the world would have been party to something as convoluted and esoteric as that?

No. All evidence points to its origins being elsewhere. Dion Fortune states the Rabbis claim that the oral tradition was first given to man by angels, and that assertion seems to be fundamental to it, but surely God would not have sent his messengers on such a commission. As I was pondering over this, the answer seemed suddenly obvious. Who, after all, was responsible for the entry of sin into the world? Who was still, as I had concluded from my researches, engaged in a struggle for world domination? Who was concerned with deceiving people, in leading them away from the true God? Satan, of course, the great deceiver himself, cast out of heaven after his rebellion and let loose on earth with those angels who had rebelled with him. It would not be God's faithful servants who taught a secret and magical system to man, but the servants of Satan, or Lucifer.

When that revelation first came to me, everything suddenly seemed to make sense. All the separate pieces of research and reading I had been doing during the past few years linked together in my mind and gave me a picture of quite startling clarity. I was able to see how mankind had been seduced from pure worship into the worship of those other gods which we read about in the Old Testament and why God had revealed himself to Abraham as the one true living God, and for the first time I understood the reason behind God's commands to the Israelites to destroy totally the pagan inhabitants of Canaan when they took possession of the land. (Deuteronomy 7:2–6). God had no illusions about the people he had chosen to set apart; he had seen their weaknesses too often during their wanderings in the desert, when they forgot the miraculous works they had seen and turned to worship pagan gods, like the golden calf in Exodus, chapter 32. He knew how easily they could be contaminated by idolatrous practices. In ordering the annihilation of all the worshippers of Baal and the Ashtoreths, the Canaanite goddesses, God was offering the Israelites a way to a completely fresh start, so that they could keep their worship pure and untainted.

They didn't take it, of course. They did not destroy all the heathen inhabitants of Canaan and thus pagan worship survived and spread insidiously to form the basis of all occultism. The Book of Judges is full of instances in which 'the children of Israel did evil in the sight of the Lord' and 'served the Baals' then repented and turned to him again for help. Each time, out of love for them, the Lord forgave them, and their fortunes rose and sank according to their relationship with him, until in 587 BC they were conquered by Nebuchadnezzar and taken into captivity in Babylon. Babylon formed the nucleus of all that was contrary to the pure worship of the living God, and was the centre of all magical practices such as spiritism, astrology, divination and witchcraft. Amongst all this the Israelites were obliged to live for some seventy years. Many fell away from the true God and began to worship Babylonian deities. Much of this is recorded in the Book of Ezekiel. Others, like Daniel, remained faithful, and the pure worship existed and developed alongside the tainted and idolatrous.

The Jews eventually returned from their exile and reformed as a nation. The walls of Jerusalem were rebuilt, as recorded in the Book of Nehemiah, and the national identity re-established. It is logical to suppose that the Kabbalism being practised by certain cults continued to exist together with the orthodox doctrine presided over by the Levitical priesthood, which ended with the destruction of the temple in AD 70. The rabbinical 'priesthood' then took the place of the Levites, and when the Jews were dispersed following the destruction of the temple by the Romans in AD 70, this secret system went with them, thus finding its way into Europe and forming the basis of many occultic practices there, including Rosicrucianism which, as shown in the preceding chapter, infiltrated and absorbed operative Freemasonry.

As I read and re-read *The Mystical Qabalah* I could only endorse F de P Castells' view that Freemasonry is indeed Kabbalism in a different garb; the similarities are unmistakable, from the reference to God as 'The Great Architect of the Universe', which most people will recognise, to the lesser-known symbols of the altar of the double cube, and the equal-armed cross which appear on the Tree of Life as symbols of Malkuth, the tenth and last Sephirah, and also form part of the ritual of the Royal Arch. It is on this altar that the 'Sacred and Mysterious Name of the True and Living God Most High' is purported to have been found. That name is revealed to the candidate as 'Jah-Bul-On'[1] and he is warned never to utter it outside the Royal Arch Chapter. Viewed in the light of what I now knew of the Kabbala, I was disturbed by the linking of God's own name, which we learn from his word is Jehovah or Yahweh (Jah) with the names of the Babylonian god Baal (Bul) and the Egyptian god Osiris (On). I now saw this for what it was, a wilful denial of him as the only true God.

The universality of Freemasonry fitted in to this syncretistic approach. All that was required of a candidate, in a religious sense, was that he should believe in a Deity, a universal deity which I myself had envisaged in earlier years, and which the Kabbalists embodied as Kether, a Sephirah on the Tree of Life. Jesus Christ had shown me exactly how misguided I had been in my approach, and that it was only through him that man could come to the

Father. In accepting him I had seen the Father at work in my life, proof, if proof were needed, of the truth of those words. It was only by coming to know Jesus personally that I had come to know God and now to recognise the blasphemy of the Kabbalistic doctrine which does not assign to Jesus his rightful place.

I should like to quote from Dion Fortune's book the two sentences which were for me the crowning proof of the blasphemy. I have mentioned earlier that on the Tree of Life, Christ appears in the sixth Sephirah, which is called Tiphareth, and that the mystic who is using this diagram must have 'unlocked' the mysteries of one Sephirah, in order to understand another. In the Kabbalistic philosophy, anyone who does not have the keys to Chesed, the fourth Sephirah, will be hallucinated in his recognition of Jesus Christ. 'He will find a personal Saviour in the God-man instead of in the regenerative influence of the Christ-force. He will worship Jesus of Nazareth as God the Father, thus confounding the Persons.' In other words, the Kabbalist is claiming that it is a Christian delusion to regard Jesus Christ as God incarnate.

When I read that I saw the Kabbala very clearly for what it was, a gross deception, something pertaining to be of God while denying the Bible; something claiming to give enlightenment while refusing to recognise the true Light of the World. There can be no way in which a professing Christian can embrace any part of such a tradition; indeed, in view of its origins, no God-fearing person, man or woman, Jew or Christian should regard it as anything other than a cult of the devil, and as such, something to be eschewed.

After I had resigned from Freemasonry, I wrote to a former 'brother' explaining my reasons in detail, and also the conclusions I had reached from my researches. This man is a Freemason of some fifty years standing, a Grand

Officer in the Craft, a 30th Degree Mason in the Rose Croix. His reply contained the following:

> I would like to know where you got the idea that there was any connection with the Kabbala or the occult. I have never heard a whisper of either. Most masons simply don't worry about such things.

I suspect the reason that most masons do not worry about such things, is that they are totally ignorant of them, as I was. They take part in the quasi-religious ceremonies without stopping to wonder about the origins of the strange words and symbols which are used. For many it becomes a substitute for religion, and the spirit of brotherhood which is engendered, as well as the many charitable works which result, gives them a sensation of being 'on the side of the angels' which is entirely fallacious. The only angels remotely connected with Freemasonry are the fallen ones who first gave the Kabbala, on which the whole thing is based, and far from being a harmless institution Freemasonry should now be seen for what it really is, a deception which leads men away from the true God rather than towards him.

In his book *Man's Inhumanity to God* David Matthews quotes the old adage that the best lies and deceits are those which have enough truth in them to deceive good men, and that highlights precisely the insidious evil of Freemasonry. Most of those involved in it are men of excellent character who genuinely believe that the organisation is nothing more than 'a system of morality'. They may pass their entire Masonic life without progressing to the higher degrees and thus never encounter anything to make them question their supposition. Had I not encountered Jesus Christ and yielded my life to him I might still be in the dark myself and I use the word 'dark' advisedly, for make no mistake, it is the Prince of Darkness himself who blinds our eyes and minds while masquerading as an 'angel of light' (2 Corinthians 4:4 and 11:14) and the 'pure light of Masonic wisdom' to which the initiate is led, is beyond doubt nothing but an acknowledgement of his sovereignty, and as such is a complete and utter counterfeit.

Note

[1] I am aware of Grand Lodge's recent statement that all reference to 'Jah-Bul-On' is to be deleted from Royal Arch ritual in the light of persistent protest. However, such a deletion cannot conceal the symbolism in both ritual and artefacts in lodge and chapter layouts, which betray the occult source of all so-called masonic wisdom and light. I can only ask readers to read carefully this and the preceding chapter once again and draw their own conclusions—or if necessary read the source material for themselves. (See bibliography.)

17

Darkness into Light

'Ian, have you repented of your sins?'

'I have.'

'Have you accepted Jesus Christ as your Saviour and will you henceforward live your life for him?'

'I will.'

'Then, Ian, in accordance with your confession of faith I now baptise you in the name of the Father, the Son and the Holy Spirit.'

I leaned backwards, supported by the arms of my Pastor and his helper. The water closed over my head and then I was being drawn up again into the warmth and light of the church. I was conscious of a feeling of great joy and peace. I was surrounded by smiling faces and as the music began and voices broke into a song of praise I joined in with a full heart:

I live, I live, because he is risen;
I live, I live, with power over sin.
I live, I live, because he is risen;
I live, I live, to worship him.
Copyright © John T Benson Pub Co, Coronation Music 1976.

Once again I was involved in ritual but this time Sally was sharing it with me and it was the ritual of baptism.

After much prayer I had realised that I could no longer remain a member of the Anglican church. I had become increasingly disturbed by the views being propounded by certain senior members of the clergy and found it less and less tolerable to listen to sermons from men who patently did not accept the Bible as the infallible word of God and their supreme authority. Liberal theology seemed to be more and more the norm, and the final crunch, as it were, came when I heard a visiting speaker dismiss the incident on the road to Emmaus, described in Luke's gospel, chapter 24, as merely allegorical.

With great sadness I explained my misgivings to our vicar and our attendances at the parish church ceased. The question of where we should go now to worship remained but in this as in other matters, we found that God was directing us. A few weeks earlier, on a pleasant Thursday evening, Sally had returned home announcing that she had 'discovered' some other Christians living very close by. We had now been some months in our rented house which was tucked away behind the High Street and approached by a pathway which adjoined the gardens of one of Mayfield's oldest houses, Yeomans. It was from there that Sally had heard the unmistakable sound of choruses being sung by live voices.

On enquiring from Betty Barefield we learned that it was the Thursday Evening Fellowship of Colkins Mill Free Church who were having their regular meeting at the home of the Pastor, Brian Hill. Soon after this discovery, when we made our decision to leave the Anglican church, I made a somewhat exploratory visit to Colkins Mill, not really knowing what a 'free' church was but interested in finding out. I discovered there a live and vibrant love of God quite unlike anything I had known before and as time went by, and I became part of this body, I experienced the practical results of this living Christianity in the love that was shown to me, a comparative stranger. Within a very short time we knew that we had found the right place and, with our children, we joined our new Christian family.

As we studied the Bible together and listened to more and more teaching from committed Christians, we concluded that the baptism we had both undergone as infants was not the same as the baptism which is taught in the gospels and that we now wished, as fully understanding adults, to undergo baptism by total immersion as a public declaration of our faith. So finally, after years of doubt, scepticism and downright muddled thinking, I found myself on 19th January 1986 standing waist-deep in warm water answering Brian's questions with a certainty I would never have dreamed of.

The succeeding years have seen great changes, both in me and in my life. As a family we have realised the truth of God's promise that he will provide for his children's needs and seen his love in action in the members of our Church Fellowship. As the lease on our rented house expired and our financial predicament grew more and more serious, a Christian friend offered a wing of their house for our use. Time and time again, when our need was desperate, money appeared with no indication of its source. The childrens' birthdays, always a source of heartache for those parents who have limited means, were made easy for us, and wonderful for the children, by the generosity of their Christian brothers and sisters.

Through another Christian, I was able eventually to begin another career, this time one in which I could use my knowledge to help other people, rather than just to prosper my own interests. Although my material wealth has diminished, I find that it no longer has the importance which it had before. God has used these years of poverty to teach me an important lesson. I have learned that Satan can use the pressures of work to prevent men particularly from seeking God or from developing their relationship with him. I have seen the folly of working just to live. God has shown me that our attitude to work should be to work to give. We should allow God to prosper us, to give us enough for ourselves and a surplus above our needs to give to others, in order to generate a God-perpetuating cycle, working to give and giving to live.

Having at last learned that lesson I have found that God is prospering us and there has been a dramatic turn for the better in my financial situation. God is fulfilling the promise which he made to me through his word, the 'Rhema' which I received soon after my meeting with Jesus:

> Your shame and disgrace are ended,
> You will live in your own land,
> And your wealth will be doubled;
> Your joy will last forever. [Good News Bible]

My priorities have changed as have my ambitions. Christian life and family life are now my prime considerations and the satisfaction which I once got from Masonic assemblies has been replaced by the deeper enjoyment of Christian meetings which are neither exclusive nor secret.

My change of direction has brought its own challenges. Family and friends have reacted to my altered lifestyle and attitudes with anything from scepticism to ridicule. They cannot refute, however, the evidence of their own eyes as they see, day by day, month by month, the Lord at work in our lives.

It was my great joy to know that my mother, after her years of searching, finally came to accept Jesus Christ as the only way to the true God. When she died I was able to conduct her funeral service at the crematorium, and my sadness at her death was lessened by the knowledge that she would now be with the Lord.

When I recall the long hours of discussion we shared, I wonder at my own blindness as I developed for myself my syncretistic faith. I thank God for Sally's years of constant prayer which God answered by revealing himself to me and now I, in my turn, pray for those whose eyes have not yet been opened to the truth of the gospel. I think of my old friends in the Brigade of Gurkhas, whom I admired and respected, and of their boisterous participation in Hindu practices; of the Tibetans who fascinated me with their gentle approach to life. I pray for them all, because Jesus died for every one of them, just as he died for me.

Above all I pray for former colleagues and friends in the Masonic movement, that they may no longer be in ignorance as to the real basis of their organisation and that the undoubted good works which Freemasons undertake, and their strong bond of brotherhood, may not blind them to the reality of what lies behind it all.

It is my heart's desire that they will learn from my experience, take heed and take stock of their lives and especially resolve to commit their lives to the Name above all names, the King of kings and Lord of lords, him in whom the fullness of the Godhead dwells bodily, the Incarnate Deity through whom the universe was made and to whom has been given all authority in heaven and earth, Christ Jesus the Lord.

Bibliography

E. M. Storms, *Should A Christian Be A Mason?*, 1980. (Foreword by Rev. James D. Shaw, former 33rd Degree Freemason) New Puritan Library Inc., 91 Lytle Road, Fletcher, NC 28732, USA. UK Distributor—Diasozo Trust, 68 Elm Road, Slade Green. Erith, Kent.

W. J. Mck. McCormick, *Christ, The Christian and Freemasonry*. Distributed by Diasozo Trust, Erith, Kent.

Walton Hannah, *Darkness Visible*. Augustine Press, 1952. Reprinted by Augustine Publishing Co. 1980.

Walton Hannah, *Christian By Degrees*. Britons Publishing Co. 1954. 4th Edn. Jan. 1964.

Freemasonry and Christianity—Are They Compatible? Prepared by the Working Group established by the Standing Committee of the General Synod of the Church of England. Church House, London.

F. de P. Castells, *The Genuine Secrets in Freemasonry*. 1978. A. Lewis (Masonic Publishers) Ltd, Shepperton, Middlesex. (Members of the Ian Allan Group)

Keith B. Jackson, *Beyond the Craft*, 1980. Lewis Masonic Publishers.

A.C.F. Jackson, CVO, CBE, 32nd Deg., *Rose Croix*. 1980. Lewis Masonic Publishers.

Illustrious Brother Brigadier A.C.F. Jackson, CVO, CBE, ADC (Retd), 33rd Deg., *A Commentary on the Rose Croix Ritual*. 1986 Edn. Lewis Masonic Publishers 1983.

E.E. Ogilvie, *Freemasons' Royal Arch Guide*. 1978. Lewis Masonic Publishers.

Roy A. Wells, *Royal Arch Matters*. 1984. Lewis Masonic Publishers.

Eugen Lennhoff, *The Freemasons*. Lewis Masonic Publishers. New Edn. 1978. First published in Germany under the title 'Die Freimaurer'. First published in Gt Britain 1934.

Alex Horne, *Sources of Masonic Symbolism*. Macoy Publishing and Masonic Supply Co. Inc., Richmond, Virginia, USA. 1981.

Bernard E. Jones, *Freemasons' Guide and Compendium*. George C. Harrap and Co., Lt. 1950. New Revised Edn. 1956. Reprinted 1977.

H. Spencer Lewis, Ph.D., F.R.C., *Rosicrucian Questions and Answers, With Complete History of the Rosicrucian Order*. Published by the Supreme Grand Lodge of AMORC, Printing and Publishing Dept., San Jose, Calif., USA. The Rosicrucian Press, San Jose, California, First Edn. 1929, Eighth Edn. 1965. Printed and bound in USA by Kingsport Press Inc., Kingsport, Tenn.

Hargrave Jennings, *The Rosicrucians, Their Rites and Mysteries*. Chatto and Windus, Piccadilly, London. 1870. Second Edn. 1879.

Arthur Edward Waite, *The Brotherhood of the Rosy*

Cross. William Rider and Son Ltd, Cathedral House, Paternoster Row, London EC4. 1924.

Max Heindel, *The Rosicrucian Cosmo-Conception on Mystic Christianity*. 1909. Renewed 1937 by Mrs Max Heindel. The Rosicrucian Fellowship, International Headquarters, Mt Ecclesia, Oceanside, California, USA. In England—L. N. Fowler and Co., Ltd, 29 Ludgate Hill, EC4.

Salem Kirban, *Satan's Angels Exposed*. Grapevine Book Distributors Inc., Rossville, GA 30741, USA. Distributed in UK by B. McCall Barbour, 28 George IV Bridge, Edinburgh.

Lady Queenborough (Edith Starr Millar), *Occult Theocrasy*. Published posthumously for private circulation only. 1933. Reprinted 1968, The Christian Book Club of America. Reprinted 1976.

Dion Fortune, *The Mystical Qabalah*. Ernest Benn Ltd, London and Tonbridge, Kent. Copyright The Society of the Inner Light 1957. First published 1935. Thirteenth impression 1979.

Manley P. Hall, *The Secret Teachings of All Ages—an Encyclopaedic Outline of Masonic, Hermetic, Qabbalistic and Rosicrucian Symbolical Philosophy; Being an Interpretation of the Secret Teachings Concealed Within the Rituals, Allegories and Mysteries of All Ages*. Printed for Manley P. Hall by H. S. Crocker Co., Inc., San Francisco, USA. 1928.

Nesta H. Webster, *Secret Societies and Subversive Movements*. First published 1924. Christian Book Club of America.

Hal Lindsey, *Satan is Alive and Well on Planet Earth*, Bantam Books USA, Zondervan 1972.

Hal Lindsey, *There's a New World Coming*. Vision House Publishers, Harvest House Publishers 1973.

Gary Allen with Larry Abraham, *None Dare Call It Conspiracy*. Introduction by Congressman John G. Schmitz. Concord Press, California, USA. 1971.

Antony C. Sutton, *Wall Street and the Rise of Hitler* and *Wall Street and the Bolshevik Revolution*. Bloomfield Books, Sudbury, Suffolk, England, in association with Heritage Publications, Melbourne, Australia, Intelligence Publications, Ontario, Canada, and Dolphin Press, Natal, South Africa.

Dan Smoot, *The Invisible Government*. Western Islands, Mass. USA. 1962. Reprinted 1977.

Rabindranath R. Maharaj, *Death of a Guru*. Hodder & Stoughton 1986.

Stephen Masood, *Into the Light*. Kingsway Publications 1986.

Bilquis Sheikh, *I Dared To Call Him Father*. Kingsway Publications 1979.

Roy Livesey, *Understanding the New Age: Preparations for Antichrist's One-World Government*. Chichester, New Wine Press 1986.